Arden's Housing Library

The Series Editors of Arden's Housing Library are **Andrew Arden QC** and **Caroline Hunter**. The team of expert authors is drawn from the members of Arden Chambers and other practitioners.

Arden's Housing Library provides accessible guidance to the details of housing rights and duties for those involved in the management of social housing. It breaks up the whole subject into digestible segments and approaches each topic from the perspective of its practical application. For our catalogue on other titles in the Library please call Lemos & Crane on 020 8348 8263 or email, admin@lemos.demon.co.uk.

Hal Pawson is a Research Fellow at the School of Housing and Planning, Heriot-Watt University, Edinburgh. **David Mullins** is a Senior Lecturer at the Centre for Urban and Regional Studies, University of Birmingham. **Siobhan McGrath** is lawyer Vice-President of the London Rent Assessment Panel and a barrister of Arden Chambers.

Allocating Social Housing

Law and Practice
in the Management
of Social Housing

Hal Pawson, David Mullins and
Siobhan McGrath

Lemos & Crane

Published in Great Britain 2000 by
Lemos & Crane
20 Pond Square
Highgate
London N6 6BA
Telephone: 020 8348 8263
Fax: 020 8347 5740
Email: admin@lemos.demon.co.uk

ISBN 1-898001-20-0

A CIP catalogue record for this book is available from the British
Library

Cover design by Blue Frog Ltd, London
Typeset by David Chapronière, London
Printed and bound by Redwood Books, Trowbridge

Contents

Table of Cases

Table of Statutes

Table of Statutory Instruments

Abbreviations

BC	Borough Council
BME	black and minority ethnic
CAP	common allocations policy
CHR	common housing register
CORE	Continuous Recording
CRE	Commission for Racial Equality
CTA	Common Travel Area
DDA	Disability Discrimination Act 1995
DETR	Department of the Environment, Transport and the Regions
EEA	European Economic Area
EOC	Equal Opportunities Commission
ERKM	ethnic record-keeping and monitoring
EU	European Union
four Es	efficiency, economy, effectiveness and equity
HA	Housing Act
HAT	Housing Action Trust
HIP	Housing Investment Programme
HOMES	Housing Organisations Mobility and Exchange Scheme
IT	information technology
LBC	London Borough Council
LCHO	low cost home ownership
MBC	Metropolitan Borough Council
NHF	National Housing Federation
reg.	regulation
RRA	Race Relations Act 1976
RSL	registered social landlord
s.	section (*pl.* ss.)
SDA	Sex Discrimination Act 1975

Acknowledgements

The authors would like to thank Caroline Hunter, Arden's Housing Library series co-editor, and Simon Latham, Community Services Director at the London Borough of Sutton, for their essential contributions and advice.

1.

The Changing Context

Introduction—allocations and social housing / The
changing allocation role / History of allocation
schemes / Scope and structure of this book / Other
sources of guidance / Future reforms for allocations
framework

Introduction—allocations and social housing

This guide is concerned with the allocation of social housing.
Some introductory comments are necessary to clarify the
contemporary meaning of both of these terms.

The term 'allocation' is commonly used in housing management in a variety of ways, sometimes to describe that part
of the rehousing process which occurs after the selection and
matching of property to applicant when an offer is accepted,
or to describe the entire rehousing process from needs assessment to offer acceptance. In line with other publications in
Arden's Housing Library, this book has a particular emphasis
on the legal concepts and provisions underlying social housing
management. In this context there is a further, more specific
meaning for 'allocation', which occurs when a new interest in
land is being created. Interestingly, this definition would
exclude transfers and assignments of tenancies from our scope
since no new interest is created. Nevertheless, the term 'allocations' has been used in its most encompassing form to cover
the entire process of finding new occupants for social housing
vacancies (including through transfers and exchanges).

The term 'social housing' also carries a variety of meanings, usually (but not always) implying housing for rent, built with public subsidy, for low income households, managed by non-profit providers. This term has been used in recent years to combine council housing, housing association, co-operative and charitable trust accommodation. Before 1988 local authorities were pre-eminent in the provision and management of social rented housing in England. While the local authority stock had already been significantly eroded by right-to-buy sales and a declining level of new build activity, it still accounted for 89 per cent of social rented housing in England in 1988. Housing associations were generally seen as complementary to local authorities during this period.

By the mid-1990s, the balance of social housing provision had begun to change, and it had become increasingly common to use the term 'social housing' to cover both local authority and housing association activity. Housing associations had become the main providers of new social rented housing and wholesale transfer of the local authority stock to housing associations had occurred in many areas in England. Elsewhere, local authorities still accounted for the vast majority of the social housing stock in their area.

From the mid-1990s new approaches have been developed to transfer poorer condition urban stock to new landlords, including provision of a new source of public funding, the Estates Renewal Challenge Fund. Local housing companies emerged as an alternative model to housing associations for such transfers. By 1998, local authorities remained the largest social housing landlord, but the proportion of social housing provided by other landlords had increased to 25 per cent in England. Some housing associations were now operating in over 200 different local authority areas—often with too small a local presence to justify keeping local waiting lists. Meanwhile, housing applicants were faced with a bewildering range of providers; this has been one stimulus to the development of common housing registers for all local social housing in some areas. All of these changes must be seen in the context of a national housing policy which placed increasing emphasis on private market provision for most needs.

Owner-occupation expanded rapidly, particularly through sales of council homes to sitting tenants. Between 1979 and 1995 the social housing stock in Britain had declined by more than a quarter, this contributing nearly half the growth in home ownership.

The 1996 Housing Act (HA 1996) introduced a change in terminology for non-profit social housing providers registered with the Housing Corporation. These landlords comprise mainly housing associations, but include other bodies such as local housing companies. Throughout this book the new term 'registered social landlord' (RSL) is used to refer to registered, non-profit social landlords, while 'social housing' is used to include RSLs and local authority housing. In 1998, there were in England approximately 1.2 million homes in the RSL sector and 4.5 million homes in the social rented sector.

The changing allocation role

The changes outlined above have transformed the role of both local housing authorities and RSLs, and brought these agencies into closer, yet more complex relationships through, for example, social housing agreements, nominations contracts, common housing registers and community care plans. However, housing policy and practice and consumer expectation have yet to fully adjust to this new situation, leading to frequent misunderstandings and frustrations. It is therefore important to consider some key changes in the context for and role of housing allocations.

Finding new occupants for social rented properties is the essential purpose of the allocations process. Landlords do not (except on very rare occasions) have the ability to search for properties to meet housing need, but do have a pressing need of their own to fill the available stock and thus avoid the costs associated with keeping properties empty. Thus, throughout the social housing field, the allocations process almost invariably involves a process of selection of the most appropriate applicants for properties as they become available. For most periods and in most areas it has been usual to define the allocations role as one of rationing as a result of the scarce supply of social housing relative to need. However, there was in the mid-1990s a more widespread recognition that some social housing no longer had a surplus demand, and indeed may be difficult, if not impossible, to let. This is introducing new and more complex considerations to allocations policy, as the latter part of this section argues.

The main impact of scarcity and rationing in housing allocations has been for landlords to establish formalised, rule-bound systems to ensure that available supply reaches those in greatest need. Much of the reforming thrust in allocations policy over the past 30 years was concerned with ensuring that 'objective' criteria were brought to bear and that the powerful 'gatekeeping' role of housing allocators was not abused. Approaches such as merit-based and date order schemes were gradually displaced by more formalised points systems.

The potential for personal intervention, in support of or in opposition to individual applicants, by councillors or by individual officers was gradually reined in. In some cases this involved 'protecting' allocations staff from direct contact with either housing management staff or the public to ensure that their decisions could be made on purely 'objective' grounds. This tendency towards a bureaucratic rationing approach continued into the 1990s, when one of the motivations for the establishment of common housing register partnerships between local authorities and RSLs was to restore needs-based rationing which had been diminished by the fragmentation of supply between a larger number of landlords. Moreover, as can be seen in the next section, HA 1996 was the most significant attempt ever to impose central government definitions of housing need on local housing allocations.

However, needs-based rationing was always challenged by a number of other tendencies. There is a tension between allocating properties on the basis of greatest housing need and meeting housing management priorities such as filling empty properties as quickly as possible. Frequently there is a difference between the urgency of rehousing need and the priority in terms of quality of accommodation allocated. There have been long-standing concerns that supposedly needs-based allocations systems often result in households with the most urgent need for housing being allocated the worst quality accommodation. Meanwhile, those with greater bargaining power as a result of less urgent needs (e.g. transfer applicants) may succeed in securing better quality accommodation.

The dominance of centralised allocations systems has been increasingly challenged by tendencies to generic housing management, with allocations tasks often undertaken by locally based estate management teams. This is particularly the case in RSLs, which rarely have the critical mass at a local level to support the degree of specialisation required for a centralised rationing approach. Inevitably, localised and generic administration of allocations has brought a wider range of considerations to bear, including the management implications of particular patterns of lettings. At the same time two further considerations have challenged traditional needs-based approaches. First, wider social changes have led to increasing concerns about the impact of needs-based allocations on quality of life of tenants in social rented estates. In the context of the residualisation of social housing, needs-based allocations are said to have produced 'unbalanced communities'. Secondly, and partly in reaction to this, a significant problem of hard-to-let social housing has begun to be recognised in parts of the country and in some localities.

Wider social changes

The promotion of owner-occupation for those who can afford to buy, and the increase in rents for those remaining, coincided with a number of wider social trends to accelerate the residualisation of social housing. The most important influence here has been change in the economy, with a sharp reduction in full-time male employment, and a predominance of part-time jobs amongst new employment opportunities. These changes were exacerbated by deregulation of the labour market, the abolition of wages councils and failure to introduce minimum wage provisions and the Social Chapter of the Maastricht Treaty by Conservative governments in the 1990s. These trends produced a growing number of households with insufficiently high or secure incomes to gain access to owner-occupation, and often forced into a housing benefit poverty trap which in turn forced them to choose between good quality but high rent social housing and no job, or a job with insufficient wages and inadequate benefit entitlement to pay the rent. These issues have been revisited by the Labour Government through initiatives on welfare to work, the minimum wage and child care provision.

Demographic change has also had a significant impact on the pattern of demand for social housing. The two most rapidly growing groups are single person households and single parent households. Both groups may be poorly placed to gain access to owner-occupation with only one salary possible, and the latter group has the added cost of child care to enable them to gain employment. As a result, both are more likely to require access to social housing than are two-adult households, including those with children. Another significant demographic trend is growth in the over-85 age group, some of whom require greater support than is traditionally available in sheltered social housing.

Another aspect of social change which has had an impact on social housing providers is the increasing number of people with mental health problems requiring housing in the community. This is partly related to policies for the closure of long-stay hospitals and the production of care plans and individual care packages by social service authorities under the National Health Service and Community Care Act 1990, but has been reflected as much (if not more) in 'normal applications' to local authority waiting lists and homeless persons sections. Between 1991 and 1994, the proportion of homeless acceptances on mental health grounds doubled from 3 to 6 per cent of all homeless applications accepted by English authorities. Some authorities had difficulties finding suitable temporary and permanent homes to allocate to these applicants, and many were using unsuitable bed and breakfast accommodation in the short term.

A further, increasingly recognised factor is the experience of 'social exclusion' by many social housing tenants and housing applicants. Low participation in employment, low household incomes and geographical segregation, and 'network poverty' may be compounded by a social stigma attaching to particular neighbourhoods and making partici-pation in wider society difficult. One manifestation of this has been the incidence of crime and anti-social behaviour, inclu-ding racial harassment, found on some social housing estates. It is argued that the majority of law-abiding tenants face further social exclusion as a result of some neighbours' beha-viour. Some authorities have sought stronger powers to evict anti-social tenants, including the use of introductory tenancies for new council tenants, and have exercised new powers to exclude such tenants from the housing register. A report by the Social Exclusion Unit in 1998 began to develop proposals for a more integrated approach, and established a series of working groups to address problems of the 'worst estates'.

Some writers have argued that bureaucratically based allocations policies have themselves played a significant role in increasing social exclusion and in inducing 'network pov-erty' by breaking up communities and weakening support networks. For example, Young and Lemos suggest that communities have been broken up and undermined by needs-based allocations policies. They recommend an 'ethical housing policy' with building communities as a central policy purpose alongside meeting housing needs. Thus, allocation policies should take account of social needs and mutual aid as well as housing need, perhaps through 'mutual aid compacts' and points for mutuality and social need.

Current policy issues

These developments have changed the context for housing allocations policies leading to new priorities such as sustainable tenancies and balanced communities which now sit alongside that of meeting housing need. These 'non-needs' influences on allocations have been reinforced by the introduction of eligibility criteria for registers by HA 1996, and changes to local priority schemes which may now exclude certain categories of applicant for consideration for permanent social housing. A related trend has been the emergence of hard-to-let housing and distinctive and innovative methods of allocating it. These factors are having a different impact in different parts of the country and in different localities. User choice (often a response to area images) has continued to interact with these and other factors to add to the variety of circumstances found across the country.

The extent of inequalities within the social housing sector are now huge. Far from seeing social housing as contributing to the achievement of citizenship rights by destroying the link between bad housing and poverty, many writers now regard occupancy of certain parts of the social housing stock as a badge of exclusion, preventing participation in wider social benefits. It is questionable whether this conjunction of circumstances can continue to be tackled by applying a single set of approaches to control access to different types of social housing in different local contexts. It seems likely that the adoption of more market-based access routes to hard-to-let housing will be combined with continued strict rationing of social housing of better quality and in more desirable areas.

History of allocation schemes

Access to social housing can be seen as a series of control processes. Table 1 (from Mullins and Niner, 1998) illustrates how control is exerted at various stages to determine who gets what, where and when. Legislation, regulation, eligibility,

Table 1. Factors controlling access to social housing

Legislation	Basic framework set by central government, e.g. extension of rights through Housing (Homeless Persons) Act 1977, reasonable preference categories for allocations schemes, and exclusion of asylum-seekers without 'recourse to public funds' in Asylum and Immigration Appeals Act 1993.
Regulation	Secretary of State, Housing Corporation etc. may set further regulations, e.g. determinations on access to statutory housing registers (under Part VI of Housing Act 1996), performance standards for Registered Social Landlords on access to housing etc., and advice, e.g. Homelessness Code of Guidance
Eligibility	Local policies may further restrict eligibility, e.g. through residence qualifications, age limits, restrictions on 'rehousing owner occupiers etc.
Prioritisation	Landlords may use variety of points schemes, group schemes, date order systems etc. to prioritise applications
Selection	Allocations systems are usually property-led. Discretion important in finding suitable applicant from prioritisation systems for given property. Factors other than need, e.g. minimising period property is empty, considering social balance of estate, may play a role at this stage.
Limited offer policies	Applicants' choice may be further restricted by limits to the number of offers they are entitled to in a given period and the way in which offers are made (usually preventing direct choices between alternatives)
Nature of housing stock	Geographical distribution, size, age and type of property play an important part in access processes. Different procedures may be applied to 'difficult to let' properties
Applicant choices	Differential bargaining power and knowledge used to exploit available choices between areas, landlords, property types etc.

Source: Mullins and Niner (1998)

prioritisation, selection and offer policies all exemplify a rationing approach with control by providers, professionals and the state. The degree of discretion available to local 'gate-keepers' is clearly constrained by the national legislative and regulatory framework. It is also influenced by local factors including the strength of the local economy and housing market and the resulting role played by social housing. Very different considerations apply in gatekeeping access to difficult-to-let housing than to housing in short supply in relation to need or demand. Considerable variations in local geographies of social housing can result.

This section briefly outlines the legislative and regulatory framework, considered in greater detail mainly in Chapters 2, 5 and 6. Prior to 1997, the legal regulation for allocation of social housing was minimal. By section 22 of HA 1985 (which re-enacted section 113(2) of HA 1957), local authorities were merely required to give a 'reasonable preference' to specified categories of persons. Such groups included those occupying insanitary or overcrowded houses, those who had large families, those living under unsatisfactory housing conditions, and the homeless.

'Reasonable preference' was not (and is not) defined or limited by statute and accordingly challenge either to an allocations policy or to a particular allocation or failure of allocation was far from easy. No statutory method of appeal to an independent tribunal or court was prescribed and therefore intervention could only be achieved through judicial review proceedings. Such proceedings placed a heavy burden on an applicant to demonstrate that an authority had acted unlawfully or irrationally. Given the open-textured nature of the phrase 'reasonable preference', it has proved difficult for applicants to enforce an individual right to be housed.

Since April 1997, allocations by a local housing authority have been governed by Part VI of HA 1996. For the first time this has imposed a detailed statutory framework on local housing authority allocations. The effect of Part VI is to impose a minimum level of uniformity in three main areas of allocation. First, it introduces the concept of 'qualifying person' and by regulation excludes specified categories of people from inclusion on a housing register (notably many of those subject to immigration control); secondly, it imposes a review procedure for those who have been refused inclusion on, or who have been removed from, the housing register (however, no right of appeal is given following a decision on internal review); and thirdly, it requires authorities to maintain an allocation 'scheme' governing both priorities and procedures.

Priorities are again circumscribed by reference to groups which must be given a 'reasonable preference', and again no right of appeal is prescribed for those dissatisfied with an allocation decision. Ultimately, therefore, the only recourse to the courts is again by way of judicial review proceedings. RSL allocations take place within the same statutory framework which governs all lettings that arise from local authority nominations. However, different considerations apply to RSL lettings other than nominations, and these are governed nationally by the Housing Corporation *Performance Standards* and may be affected locally by participation in common housing registers.

Case study research carried out for Shelter in May/June 1997 on the early impacts of the legislation (Niner, 1997) looked at issues of citizenship rights and local authority discretion in this new context. On the surface at least, the rights of the homeless *vis-à-vis* other applicants for social housing were fundamentally changed by the Act in such a way as to remove any structured channel for 'fast track' access. However, the research showed that most authorities had tried with some ingenuity to devise their Part VI priority schemes so as to replicate as far as possible the pre-existing balance between 'homeless' and other applicants in allocations, using the new reasonable preference categories. Partly this was driven by the need to keep control of the amount and cost of temporary (two-year duty) accommodation needed, but there seems also to have been recognition that homeless people merit priority because of their needs. Despite initial fears of increased Secretary of State prescription, the new legislation seemed in the event to have enlarged the scope for local authority discretion.

In November 1997, regulations were introduced to modify homelessness and access policies so that people owed a homelessness duty would again become a reasonable preference category for allocations, and any accommodation used under section 197 must be available for at least two years. These provisions restored some of the homelessness rights removed in 1996, and further review was promised.

Scope and structure of this book

This book provides an account of legislation, regulation and practice in the field of social housing allocations in England. In general, the intended audience is housing staff with practical responsibilities covering aspects of the allocation process. Some parts of the book, particularly Chapters 7 and 8, may be of particular interest to housing policy-makers.

The book forms part of Arden's Housing Library, and benefits from expert legal input; it should be read in conjunction with previously published volumes on related subjects (such as tenants' rights, dealing with issues such as succession and assignment of tenancies). It shares the series' perspective that the influence of law can only be fully appreciated by examining the ways in which the law comes to be applied, understood and accepted and by exploring how it works in practice. The book is also, therefore, founded on extensive research undertaken by two of the authors in the field of housing policy and practice.

The geographical scope of the publication is confined to England and Wales (because of the very different legal provisions, policy and context found elsewhere in the United Kingdom). Its sectoral scope extends to social housing, defined here as rented housing provided by local authorities and RSLs. This requires examination of the two different legal and regulatory frameworks applying to English local authorities and RSLs. The aim is to journey through the territory thus defined, highlighting key legal, policy and practice issues of relevance to housing managers.

In the management of social housing a significant distinction may be made between 'general needs' housing on the one hand, and 'special needs' or 'supported' housing on the other. In terms of housing allocations, much of the legal and regulatory framework is commonly applicable. To this extent, the book is as relevant to those concerned with specialist accommodation as it is to those managing mainstream housing. Certain sections within Chapters 2, 4 and 6 are, however, possibly of specific interest. Examples include the discussion of routes into social housing for people needing adapted housing or support (see Chap. 2), the role of home visits in assessing the impact of ill health and/or disability on rehousing requirements (see Chap. 4), and the regulatory expectations of the Housing Corporation as regards lettings policies for supported housing (see Chap. 6).

Chapter 2 provides an overview of access for new tenants to social housing, considering each of the main access routes and the ways in which landlords filter applications, principally through the housing registers established by local authorities under HA 1996. It goes on to discuss the legal and regulatory framework and the operation of discretion. Chapter 3 mirrors the issues covered in Chapter 2, this time considering the ways in which existing tenants move between properties within the social housing sector. While such moves account for well over a third of lettings, considerably less legal and policy attention has been devoted to them.

Chapter 4 introduces the next section of the book, which considers allocations systems, their rationale and the ways in which they measure housing need. This chapter also discusses the ways in which systems are being adapted to address factors other than housing need, such as marketing unpopular properties and promoting 'balanced communities'. The allocation of local authority housing is considered in greater detail in Chapter 5 by examining the specific provisions of

Parts VI and VII of HA 1996. Meanwhile Chapter 6 considers the special considerations applying to RSL allocations, drawing on the regulatory guidance provided by the Housing Corporation's *Performance Standards*.

Chapter 7 considers the inextricable links between the allocations task and the exercise of discrimination (i.e. certain applicants are selected, while others are refused), and the necessity of ensuring that this does not extend to unlawful discrimination. The chapter therefore defines unlawful discrimination with reference in particular to race and sex discrimination and discrimination against those with disabilities, and identifies how these may arise in relation to allocations. It goes on to explore the ways in which such discrimination can be countered and equal opportunities applied in allocations; it considers both legal redress and policy and practice initiatives which landlords should undertake, such as ethnic record-keeping and monitoring.

Finally, Chapter 8 discusses the ways in which social landlords can monitor the allocations process to ensure that their policy and procedural objectives are achieved in practice and to inform future policy development. It also deals with the legal provisions concerning fraudulent applications.

Other sources of guidance

This is a practical guide, not an academic text. For this reason, academic referencing has generally been avoided. However, for the benefit of readers who wish to pursue some of the issues in greater depth, suggested further reading is included at the end of each chapter. Some of the publications cited here have been drawn on as 'source material' for the main body of the text.

Perhaps the single most important item of further reading is the DETR's *Code of Guidance on Allocations and Homelessness*. Although a Code on homelessness has existed for many years, the inclusion of allocations dates only from 1997, following the HA 1996. At the time of writing, the *Code* is under review. A draft revised edition was produced for consultation in 1999 and this incorporated significant changes in emphasis by comparison with the previous version.

Unfortunately, it has not proved possible to synchronise publication of this guide with that of the fully revised *Code*. For this reason, we have had to use the 1999 draft revised edition as the basis for referencing. Our citations of specific paragraphs refer to this version of the document and may not be wholly consistent with the fully revised edition due for publication in 2000. Nevertheless, with respect to allocations, it is understood that the substance of the draft document will be very largely or wholly reflected in the revised text.

Future reforms for allocations framework

As this book goes to press, a review of housing policy in England and Wales is under way, as a prelude to the publication of the first Housing Policy Green Paper for over 20 years. Allocations and homelessness policies are particularly under the spotlight and there are indications that far-reaching reforms are being contemplated. It is, however, unlikely that the parliamentary timetable will allow new legislation to be considered by Parliament before the next election. Bearing this in mind, it seems highly likely that the current legislative and regulatory framework will remain largely intact for some years to come.

Further reading

Mullins, D. (1998). 'More Choice in Social Rented Housing'. In D. Mullins and A. Marsh (eds), *Housing and Public Policy. Citizenship, Choice and Control*, pp. 124–152. Milton Keynes: Open University Press.

Mullins, D. and Niner, P. (1998). 'A Prize of Citizenship? Changing Access to Social Housing'. In D. Mullins and A. Marsh (eds), *Housing and Public Policy. Citizenship, Choice and Control*, pp. 175–198. Milton Keynes: Open University Press.

Niner, P., with White, V. and Levison, D. (1997). *The Early Impacts of the 1996 Housing Act and Housing Benefit Changes*. London: Shelter.

Page, D. (1993). *Building for Communities. A Study of New Housing Association Estates*. York: Joseph Rowntree Foundation.

Pawson, H. and Kearns, A. (1998). 'Difficult to Let Social Housing Association Stock in England: Property, Management and Context'. In *Housing Studies* 13:4.

Young, M. and Lemos, G. (1997). *The Communities We Have Lost and Can Regain*. London: Lemos & Crane.

2.
Access to Social Housing

Housing advice and publicity / The housing register and regulation of access to social housing / Special categories of applicants / Maintenance of local authority housing registers / Access to housing association tenancies / Rights to information on part of social housing applicants / Common housing registers

To a great extent access to social housing is regulated by local housing authorities which are under a variety of duties and have various powers. Part VI of HA 1996 sets the framework for local housing authority allocation, including the rules on those disqualified from access to the housing register. Part VII governs the duties towards the homeless. Additional duties towards specified groups are imposed on local authorities by a variety of statutes including the National Assistance Act 1948, the Children Act 1989 and the National Health Service and Community Care Act 1990.

Although most RSLs maintain their own waiting lists, allocation to tenancies often follows nomination by a local authority. If requested by the local authority, all RSLs are required to co-operate to a reasonable extent in offering accommodation to people with priority on the authority's waiting list (HA 1996, s. 170).

For most people, gaining access to social housing comes about through application to a local authority. Customarily, the queue of applicants has been termed the 'waiting list'. The impression given is that the queue is prioritised largely according to the length of time that applicants have been registered. Nowadays, whilst waiting time continues to be a factor in many systems (see Chap. 4), priority tends to be determined mainly according to measures of need. For this reason, and also because the term 'housing register' is given a statutory meaning in HA 1996, this term is used here in preference to 'waiting list'.

This chapter examines each route of access into social housing, and explains how social landlords process and filter applications from individuals seeking a tenancy. It discusses the legal and regulatory framework within which landlords operate with respect to access, and describes some of the ways in which available discretion within the law is exercised.

It is worth bearing in mind that, given limited rehousing resources and differing applicant needs and requirements, it can be a mistake to regard the access process as being simply about selecting new tenants for social landlords. Application systems can be adapted to meet a much wider range of needs. For example, where local authorities operate rent deposit schemes and other processes managing access to better quality private rented accommodation, they may use their housing register as a means of identifying and targeting potential users. The same applies to low cost home ownership (LCHO) initiatives which can be targeted on better-off applicants who may stand little chance of a social sector tenancy. Meanwhile, housing assessments often need to be integrated with wider assessments of care and support needs (see pp. 34–35) if relevant solutions are to be found to the overall needs of applicants.

Housing advice and publicity

Housing advice and publicity are means by which social landlords may solicit tenancy applications from people in need of accommodation.

Section 179 of HA 1996 requires every local authority to 'secure that advice and information about homelessness, and the prevention of homelessness is available free of charge to any person in their district'. Authorities are expected to develop housing advice strategies as part of their overall local housing strategy in partnership with other agencies, social landlords and the private sector. The Act also provides for authorities to fund other agencies contributing in the comprehensive local advice service. While the legal requirement specifically relates to homelessness, good practice guidance suggests that the duty should be interpreted more widely to include comprehensive advice on social housing, the private rented sector and home ownership; and these services should be integrated with welfare rights and debt advice. More generally, local authority powers to provide information to citizens on their own services are conferred by section 142 of the Local Government Act 1972.

Often, the main focus of specialist housing advice teams and agencies involves accessing accommodation opportunities, protecting tenants' occupancy and maintaining standards in the private sector. Nevertheless, virtually all local authorities which maintain a landlord role (and some which do not) offer advice on how to register for local authority housing. In most cases, help with applying for housing association tenancies is also on hand. Generally, such assistance takes the form of explanatory leaflets and, in some cases, advice offered through home visits. In the context of discrimination (see Chap. 7), it is important to recognise that housing advice may be the first point of contact for a potential housing applicant, and applications which do not proceed beyond this point are unlikely to be recorded through systems linked to the housing register. Landlords operating in areas where there are significant numbers of non-English speakers often translate leaflets into appropriate languages to ensure that people unfamiliar with the social housing system are not denied access.

With social housing vacancies in relatively short supply, landlords have seen it as neither necessary nor appropriate to solicit applicants through active publicity (e.g. advertising). Increasingly in recent years, however, both local authorities and RSLs in many parts of the country have found that particular blocks, estates and areas have become increasingly difficult to let (see Chap. 4). Generating a body of applicants for vacancies in areas of this kind has required a more proactive approach. Such marketing can take many forms. These include advertising vacancies in the local press, opening premises similar to an estate agency in a town centre, or designating a flat as a show home to demonstrate the positive characteristics of a property (particularly where small size is perceived to be a problem).

The housing register and regulation of access to social housing

Local authority housing register

Under section 162 of HA 1996, every local authority must establish and maintain a housing register containing the names of people eligible to be rehoused into council housing or (through a nomination) into an RSL tenancy. Although an authority may contract out the role of running its housing register, it remains the authority's duty to ensure that the register is maintained in accordance with the statute (draft revised *Code of Guidance*, ch. 21).

For most people seeking a tenancy in social rented housing, the housing register is a gateway through which they must pass. As far as applicants who are not already local authority or RSL tenants are concerned, this holds true for all social rented sector tenancies other than 'direct applicant' allocations by RSLs (see below). In general, for each application entered on the register, a local authority will record a range of details about the applicant's housing needs and preferences to facilitate:

- ranking the applicant's rehousing priority, and
- matching the applicant's requirements against the characteristics of properties available for letting at the appropriate time.

Regulations also specify that each register entry must include the applicant's address, the date on which the application was originally added to the register and the most recent date on which the entry was amended.

Meeting the cost of the register

The cost of operating the register falls within the statutory Housing Revenue Account as a matter of management of an authority's stock, since 'management of houses and other property' in this context has a wide enough meaning to include the selection of tenants (*Shelley v London County Council* (1948)). As such the costs must be met within the ring-fenced account (see Local Government and Housing Act 1989, s. 74 and Sched. 4). The costs of assessment of homeless persons, prior to a decision that they are unintentionally homeless and therefore 'qualifying persons' for the register (see below), do not, however, fall within the costs that should be debited to the account as they are not part of the management of the stock (*R v Ealing LBC, ex p Lewis*(1992)).

Qualifying persons

The HA 1996 introduced the concept of 'qualifying persons' for housing register registration purposes. Under the Act, certain categories of persons are disqualified from access to the register (s. 161). Subject to those classes ('statutory exclusions'), local authorities have discretion over who should and should not qualify for registration. However, authorities should not have *rigid* policies in operating their housing waiting lists. Therefore, although an authority may specify categories of persons who can or cannot qualify for an allocation, it should generally allow for exceptions from any strict criteria. However, where discretion is used to exclude certain potential applicants it is important that this is monitored so that those responsible are accountable (see Chap. 8).

Statutory exclusions and inclusions: legal framework

Immigration control

Generally, those who are subject to immigration control are disqualified from being eligible for inclusion on the housing register. This covers all non-British, non-EU nationals, including all asylum seekers and people subject to sponsorship undertakings within the previous five years or whose sponsor is no longer alive. However, particular groups of persons have been brought back within eligibility (Allocation of Housing Regulations 1996 (S.I. No. 2753—the 1996 Regulations), reg. 4). Under these provisions the following qualify:

1. refugees (Class A);
2. persons who have been granted exceptional leave to enter or remain, and the leave is not subject to a condition requiring maintenance and accommodation without recourse to public funds (Class B);
3. persons habitually resident in the Common Travel Area (CTA) with current leave to enter or remain which is not subject to any limitation or condition except on the basis that a sponsor who is still alive will be responsible for maintenance and accommodation, and there has been residence of less than five years (Class C); and
4. persons habitually resident in the CTA who are nationals of a state which is a signatory to the European Convention on Social and Medical Assistance or the Council of Europe Social Charter and who is habitually resident in the CTA (Class CA).

Also, persons who are European Economic Area (EEA) nationals who are required by the Secretary of State to leave the United Kingdom are not eligible (1996 Regulations, reg. 5).

The CTA comprises the United Kingdom, the Republic of Ireland, the Isle of Man and the Channel Islands; the EEA covers EU countries, Iceland, Norway and Liechtenstein. See generally paragraphs 4.7–4.13 of the *Code of Guidance to Parts VI and VII of the Housing Act 1996*.

Habitual residence

Even British and EU nationals who are not actually habitually resident in the CTA are also not qualifying persons. Habitual residence is not defined, but means that an applicant has lived in the CTA for an appreciable period of time, has a firm intention to continue to reside there and that intention is viable. Note that some classes of person are to be *treated* as being habitually resident, such as persons who are workers for the purpose of EEC regulations and persons with a right to reside in the United Kingdom pursuant to relevant Council directives (1996 Regulations, reg. 6).

Homelessness

Special provision is made for the homeless as defined under Part VII of HA 1996. Two categories of homeless households are to be regarded as being eligible for inclusion on the housing register:

1. people over age 18 who have been found to be homeless or threatened with homelessness, in priority need and not intentionally homeless; and
2. people over age 18 who in the past two years have been found to be homeless or threatened with homelessness, not intentionally homeless but also not in priority need.

For the second group, eligibility may lapse if there has been a subsequent finding of intentionality.

Whilst homeless people in the categories defined above are *always* qualifying persons in terms of the statutory exclusions, there are concerns that some authorities may defer the applications of certain homeless households under their discretionary powers (see below). The way that homeless applicants are incorporated within systems of rehousing prioritisation under the HA 1996 framework is discussed in Chapter 5.

Statutory exclusions and inclusions: operation of legislation

In practice, the impact of the statutory exclusions discussed above varies substantially between authorities, depending on the extent to which the area is a frequent destination for asylum seekers and others subject to immigration control. Consequently, the effects are generally greatest in the London area. In implementing this aspect of the legislation, local authorities routinely may ask applicants directly whether they are covered by any of the specified exclusions. An alternative approach is to require all applicants to provide comprehensive details of their recent housing history, with further questions being triggered according to responses.

Complexities arise because, in the past, housing officers have not needed to be well-versed in immigration law. Problems also result from the fact that, for many of the applicants involved, English is not a first language.

Discretionary exclusions

Aside from the statutory exclusions and inclusions specified in law, section 161(4) of HA 1996 also gives local authorities substantial discretionary powers to determine their own policies for who qualifies for housing and who does not. The *Code of Guidance* generally advocates a cautious approach to the specification of groups subject to discretionary exclusion from the housing register. For example, with respect to framing exclusion rules relating to anti-social behaviour, authorities are advised to consult with relevant criminal justice agencies (e.g. the police and the probation service). More generally, authorities devising exclusion policies to any group are recommended to discuss their proposals with a range of other agencies including health authorities, RSLs and voluntary groups (draft revised *Code of Guidance*, para. 3.11).

The *Code* also contains specific advice on discretionary exclusion on the grounds of rent arrears (draft revised *Code*, para. 3.18). Authorities are advised against simply excluding all persons who owe rent or who have a history of incurring arrears. Instead, rules should be framed in such a way that they take account of housing needs, and of an applicant's commitment to pay off debt. It is further argued that housing register eligibility policies should take no account of non-housing debts which an applicant might have incurred. Case-law has, in any event, shown that criteria unrelated to housing matters (e.g. local taxation arrears) may be unlawful (*R v Forest Heath DC, ex p West and Lucas* (1991)).

Whatever general rules local authorities use to define who can appear on the register, they are encouraged to make provision to enable others to appear if their individual circumstances merit it. This is especially important for vulnerable people with a particular need for settled housing, but there could be exceptional cases across the whole range of potential applicants. The general point is that local authorities should not adopt 'blanket bans' of particular classes of applicants: allocation procedures must allow for genuine discretion in individual cases.

> **Case report: Considering each application on its merits**
>
> The applicant held a joint secure tenancy in Thanet with her cohabitee. Following the breakdown of their relationship she moved to Canterbury and applied for accommodation there. Initially, the council refused to accept her onto the waiting list until she relinquished the secure tenancy, which she was unable to do because of outstanding rent arrears. The applicant started judicial review proceedings and the council agreed to consider her application. However, on receipt of that application, the council decided that the

> applicant could not be rehoused while she retained an interest in the secure tenancy. The decision was quashed on the basis that it constituted a rule rather than a general approach subject to exceptions which would permit each application to be separately considered. *R v Canterbury City Council, ex p Gillespie* (1987)

In practice, local authority action on discretionary exclusions takes two forms. On the one hand, a group may be simply prohibited from registration on the housing register. On the other, an authority may specify classes of persons who are allowed to register, but who cannot be made a secure tenancy offer within their own stock or a nomination to an RSL unless their designation is changed or until a specified period expires (see Chap. 4). Examples of the kinds of categories specified under these powers include:

- Persons with a record of anti-social behaviour
- Persons with rent arrears
- Owner-occupiers
- Persons not resident in the authority
- Persons below a specified minimum age
- Persons whose incomes and/or savings exceed given threshold(s)
- RSL tenants
- Squatters
- Applicants with no assessed housing need
- Households previously found to be 'intentionally homeless'.

The groups excluded from registration under discretionary powers (see above) tend to fall into three overall categories. First, there are those considered to have committed offences or to have been 'unsatisfactory tenants'. This would include those evicted because of anti-social behaviour or with a record of rent arrears (see e.g. *R v Wolverhampton MBC, ex p Watters* (1997)). Exclusions of this sort are partly motivated by a wish to deter other potential offenders. Groups such as owner-occupiers and those on moderate or high incomes form a second category of applicants often excluded from housing registers on discretionary grounds. This is justified by a view that such households should be able to satisfy their housing needs in other tenures. Thirdly, there are those such as out-of-area temporary accommodation placements, housing association tenants and very young people (e.g. under age 18) who may be excluded on the basis that they are the responsibility of another authority, landlord or agency.

The legislation gives no guidance on the period over which an exclusion owing to 'an offence' should continue to apply to a particular applicant or class of applicants; the draft revised *Code of Guidance*, though, states that exculsion should not be in perpetuity (para. 3.18). In some cases, local authorities specify the length of time following an incident or judgment during which an exclusion will apply. For example, in the case of an eviction owing to anti-social behaviour or rent arrears, this might last for two years. A relevant point is that some criminal convictions become spent or ignored after a certain period. There is no requirement for ex-offenders to disclose spent convictions and they have no direct bearing on housing need. However, custodial sentences of more than two-and-a-half years are never spent.

Housing Corporation regulatory guidance for RSLs specifies that events prompting a landlord to exclude an applicant must have occurred within two years of the person's application.

Discretionary exclusions—sex offenders

Authorities seeking to define classes of person as not qualifying for housing on the grounds of previous anti-social behaviour need to focus on risk assessments by specialist agencies such as the police or probation service, rather than on their own judgements, or simply on the nature of the offence itself. This applies in particular to decisions about members of groups such as sex offenders. Good practice advice suggests that sex offenders' housing applications should be considered alongside those of others whose past or present behaviour may pose a high level of risk to members of the community where they settle, should they re-offend. A sex offender may pose some risk to local people, particularly if supervision arrangements are inadequate. Nevertheless, it is likely to be in the interests of community safety for the applicant to be rehoused where he or she can be monitored, rather than being excluded and pushed towards an unsupervised tenancy in the private sector (see also Chap. 4).

The interaction between Parts VI and VII of HA 1996 (see p. 86 below) needs to be kept in mind by authorities minded to prevent access to social housing on the part of groups such as sex offenders and others with a history of anti-social behaviour. Whilst authorities retain considerable discretion over who is allowed access to housing registers, households deemed to be homeless within the terms of Part VII have a special status in this regard (see p. 32). A former sex offender found to be unintentionally homeless and in priority need has a right to be entered on the register, irrespective of an authority's general policies as regards Part VI housing applicants.

Operation of housing register

Applications

A person who applies for housing and is a qualifying person must be put on the register (HA 1996, s. 163(1)), but the authority may enter others (e.g. homeless applicants) without application (s. 163(2)). In either event the person must be notified (s. 163(3)). Authorities may amend entries, and again must notify the applicant if they do so (s. 163(4)).

Example: Information to be contained in housing register

The register must contain the following information:

1. Qualifying person's name

2. Number of other persons who normally reside with him or her as a member of his or her family or who might reasonably be expected to reside with him or her

3. Number of persons who are:
- under the age of 10 years,
- expecting child, or
- over the age of 60 years.

4. Qualifying person's address

5. Date on which the qualifying person was put on the register

6. Most recent date on which an entry on the register was amended.

(See HA 1996, s. 162(4) and the 1996 Regulations, reg. 7.)

Removal

A person may be removed from the register in such circumstances as the authority thinks fit. A person *must* be removed if it appears that he or she has never been or is no longer a qualifying person. If an applicant makes a request to be removed from the register, the authority must do so *unless* that person is one towards whom the main homelessness duties are owed (s. 163(5), (6)).

Before removal there must be notification in accordance with regulations. Under regulation 8(2) of the 1996 Regulations, the authority must:
1. require the person to provide such information as it reasonably requires;
2. specify a period of not less that 28 days beginning with the day on which the person receives the notice within which the information must be provided; and
3. inform the person that it may decide to remove him or her from its register:
   - if it does not receive the information, or

- if it considers that in the light of the information provided there are reasons why he or she should be removed.

The notice must be in writing, and if not received shall be treated as having been given if it is made available at the authority's office for a reasonable period for collection by him or her (reg. 8(3)).

Reviews

If an authority decides not to include an applicant on, or decides to remove an applicant from, the register, the applicant must be notified of the decision together with reasons (s. 164(1)). The purpose of the requirement to give reasons has been said to be to enable the recipient to establish whether this action might be challengeable in law. In *R v Northampton BC, ex p Carpenter* (1993) (decided under the homelessness legislation) the purpose of the section was said to be 'to enable someone who is entitled to a decision to see what the reasons are for that decision and to challenge those reasons if they are apparently inadequate'. In that case, a family moved from secure accommodation in Edinburgh where it had lived on a council estate where there were severe drug problems. The family applied for accommodation in Northampton but its application was rejected on the basis that it had made itself intentionally homeless. No reasons for the decision were given other than that regard had been given to the general circumstances prevailing in Edinburgh. The court decided that although it was not necessary for an authority to deal with every written allegation, it was not open to it to say that the general statement provided amounted to adequate reasons.

More recently, in the context of the right to seek an internal review, it has been said that the purpose 'is to enable the applicant to put before the local housing authority a proper case based upon a full understanding of the council's previous decision to refuse accommodation' (per Latham J in *R v Camden LBC, ex p Mohammed* (1998)).

> **Case report: removal of applicants from housing register**
>
> An application had been removed from the register by the local authority following the refusal of what was deemed to be a 'reasonable offer' of accommodation. The applicant had objected to being offered a bedsit rather than a larger dwelling. The council informed the applicant that his application would be suspended for a two-year period. Although the notification informed the applicant of reasons for the decision, it failed to refer to the recommendation made by the council's Social Services Department that the applicant needed a property containing separate rooms for living and sleeping. On that basis, it was held that the decision letters 'fail[ed] to provide adequate reasons for the offer being made for bedsit accommodation, rather than the living room plus bedroom accommodation for which the applicant had been applying'. *R v Westminster City Council, ex p Nadhum Husain* (1998)

The decision notice must also inform the applicant of the right to request a review of the decision and of the time within which such a request must be made (s. 164(2)).

A review under section 164 must be requested within 21 days of the decision being notified to the applicant or within a longer period if the authority agrees in writing. The decision whether to extend time is for the authority alone. Refusal can only be challenged by judicial review. Once a request has been properly made a review *must* be carried out (s. 164(3)).

Under S.I. 1999 No. 71, an authority receiving a request for a review (under s. 164) must notify the applicant that he or she (or someone acting on his or her behalf) may make written representations in connection with the review, and must also provide the applicant with details of the review procedure to be followed. Any representations submitted must be considered. Subsequently, the authority must notify the applicant of its decision within eight weeks of the original request (unless a longer period is agreed between the two parties).

There is no statutory appeal against the decision made by the authority following the review procedure. The only possible challenge is by way of judicial review.

Special categories of applicants

There is a number of groups which have special legal status in relation to registration on the housing register and, hence, access to social housing. These include homeless households, children in need, other vulnerable persons, persons with community care needs, and those displaced because of compulsory purchase.

Homelessness

The statutory provisions relating to the homeless are dealt with in Part VII of HA 1996 (replacing Part III of HA 1985). Parts VI and VII of HA 1996 interrelate to achieve the stated purpose of Parliament that there should be only one route to obtaining access to local authority housing and for nominations to RSLs.

A person who is assessed by the housing authority as homeless, in priority need and not intentionally homeless will therefore join the unified housing register, rather than being allocated housing as a priority over others. However, the fact of their homelessness means that they too must be afforded a 'reasonable preference'.

Whilst awaiting an allocation, homeless persons have the right to be provided with interim accommodation either from the authority's own stock (in which case they will not be secure tenants) or by arrangement with other social or private sector landlords (in which case, they will be assured shorthold, rather than assured, tenants). Temporary accommodation provided by a local authority must be for a maximum period of two years, with the applicant's case being reassessed at the end of that time. All these issues are covered in more detail in Chapter 5.

Children in need

Under section 20 of the Children Act 1989, a local *social services* authority must provide accommodation for a child in its area who requires it as a result of:
1. there being no person who has parental responsibility for the child;
2. the child having been lost or abandoned; or
3. the person who has been caring for the child being prevented from providing him or her with suitable accommodation.

Accommodation must also be provided for any child who has reached age 16 and whose welfare the authority considers is likely to be seriously prejudiced if it does not provide him or her with accommodation.

In discharging these duties a social services authority may ask the local housing authority for assistance (Children Act 1989, s. 27) and the housing authority *must* comply with the request to the extent that it is compatible with its own statutory duties and other obligations and does not unduly prejudice the discharge of any of its own functions.

Where a child needs accommodation because his or her family has become homeless, recourse may be had to Part VII of HA 1996. But if there is already a determination that the family is *intentionally* homeless, the housing authority is under no duty to house and may lawfully refuse to assist under section 27 (*Smith v Northavon DC* (1994)). In such circumstances the social services authority would retain responsibility. (See also J. Henderson, *Children and Housing* (Arden's Housing Library, 2000).)

Other vulnerable persons

Under section 21 of the National Assistance Act 1948, social service authorities have a duty to provide residential accommodation for people in need of care or attention which is not otherwise available to them, on account of age, illness, disability or other circumstances. The duty extends to providing assistance, for example, to those who are too mentally disabled to make an application as homeless (see *ex p Begum*, [add citation]).

The section was also applied to in-country asylum seekers who are otherwise destitute, because they are not entitled to welfare benefits or assistance under Part VII of HA 1996 (*R v Newham LBC, ex p Gorenkin* (1998)). However, since 4 February 1998, local housing authorities have been permitted to house those asylum seekers owed accommodation duties under the National Assistance Act or the homelessness legislation or who are children in need.

Community care

The National Health Service and Community Care Act 1990 requires social services departments to carry out an assessment for any individual who may have a need for community care services, including housing. If there is a housing need, section 47 requires social service authorities to notify the housing authority, where appropriate housing could then be allocated under Part VI of HA 1996. The draft revised *Code of Guidance* suggests that housing and social service authorities should 'liaise closely over the best solution for each client' and agree a joint approach as to mechanisms for referral between departments, co-ordination, communication and follow-up, the assessment of individuals who require emergency accommodation and the identification of those with inter-dependent health, housing and social service needs (para. 2.15).

Community care assessments raise important practical implications for housing advice providers. By focusing on users' needs in an holistic way, it is clear that rehousing needs cannot always be separated from care and support needs. Research suggests that this is true of a much wider group than those who receive formal community care assessments. For example, older people having difficulty living in their present accommodation have needs which might be addressed by rehousing; they might equally be addressed by staying put where necessary adaptations and repairs are made to their property and care services provided. Such complex needs are often inadequately addressed by traditional rehousing applications procedures which 'put the product before the person'. For example, some local authorities still assume that any housing applicant aged over 60 is applying for sheltered housing; while this assumption may help to fill vacancies, it may not accord with user preferences.

There is a number of routes into social housing for people needing adapted housing or support. These include:

1. the housing register, with priority being determined on the basis of the applicant's current housing circumstances, a medical assessment, and information supplied by other relevant agencies such as social services;
2. referral quotas made available mainly to social services departments;
3. acceptance as a 'vulnerable person' under Part VII of HA 1996 (homelessness), with the decision informed by a medical assessment; and
4. 'fast track' arrangements for dealing with emergencies outside the 'normal' system and occasionally brought into play in cases of urgent medical need.

As the *Code of Guidance* makes clear, persons subject to quota arrangements must fall within the remit of at least one of the 'reasonable preference' criteria (see p. 82 below). It is also a requirement that 'quota referral' allocations involve persons whose names appear on the statutory housing register (see pp. 20–32 above).

Compulsory purchase

Under section 39 of the Land Compensation Act 1973, housing authorities may be under a duty to rehouse residential occupiers displaced from accommodation as a result of compulsory purchase. Allocation under this duty does not fall within the ambit of Part VI of HA 1996 (1996 Regulations, reg. 3).

Maintenance of local authority housing registers

The needs and aspirations of people applying for social housing are liable to change fairly frequently. As a result, the accuracy of recorded information decays rapidly. Partly for this reason, it is essential that housing registers are reviewed on a frequent or continuous basis, and that applicants are encouraged to report changes of circumstances when they occur. Such reviews involve verification of applicants' circumstances and confirmation of whether they have a continuing interest in obtaining a tenancy. Maintaining an up-to-date register is of direct benefit to local authorities as landlords, because it minimises the proportion of tenancy offers which fail, either because they were sent to the wrong address or because the applicant was no longer in need of housing. Cutting down on failed offers helps to control void rates.

In practice there are two main approaches to reviewing registers. Most commonly, authorities periodically review their entire list—usually annually—whilst in about a quarter of authorities the register is under continuous review. This involves re-contacting individual applicants periodically, such as on the anniversary of their application and annually thereafter. Where an applicant fails to respond to a review letter, the usual practice is to remove the name from the register. This is sometimes referred to as 'cutting out the dead wood'.

Reviewing applications is one of a number of quality control measures which should be routinely adopted to make best use of housing registers. Other measures include ensuring that data input is verified (either on a sample basis, or by 'double key-entry'), that target times are set and monitored for recording new applications, undertaking 'bypass monitoring' to ensure that high priority applications are not overlooked, and targeted mailings (e.g. to applicants who might be interested in LCHO opportunities). Chapter 8 considers some of these issues further, while the implications of the Data Protection Act for accuracy of and access to records held on housing registers are considered later in this chapter.

Access to housing association tenancies

Background

The RSL sector accommodates a substantial and increasing proportion of those moving into social housing. In practice, about half of all new tenants housed by RSLs access the sector through a nomination from a local authority (see below). To this extent, the procedures for regulating access to local authority housing registers described above affect who is eligible for an offer of an RSL tenancy. However, this still leaves significant numbers of RSL tenancies which are allocated either to people who apply direct to an association, or to households referred by voluntary or other statutory agencies.

Regulatory framework

RSLs are regulated by the Housing Corporation which has issued (pursuant to its power under section 36A of the Housing Associations Act 1985) prescriptive guidance known as *Performance Standards* (the third edition of which incorporates statutory management guidance under section 36 of HA 1996). These standards are now divided into three 'Governance and Finance Standards' and six 'Social Housing Standards'. For regulation purposes associations must, on an annual basis, confirm compliance with these requirements through a self-certification process (Annual Regulatory Return), and may need to demonstrate the validity of this certification on Housing Corporation follow-up visits.

Social Housing Standard F deals with lettings and specifies that 'RSLs should normally let their homes to people in greatest housing need'. Their lettings and policies should be independent, fair, accountable, and make the best use available stock; they should aim to let tenancies which are sustainable in the long term and contribute to stable communities.

A number of compliance tests are specified for this standard and further interpretation of each of these is set out in the *Performance Standards* (Housing Corporation, 1997). The main requirements are set out below, while Chapter 6 discusses some of them in greater detail. RSLs must:
- Have written lettings policies
- Consult with local authorities on intended changes to these
- Make policies publicly available on request
- Monitor lettings and review policies to ensure that the selection and allocation process is effectively controlled and accurately recorded
- Let homes in ways that are fair and non-discriminatory
- Avoid irrelevant restrictions on access
- Give reasonable preference to those in housing need except where this would lead to unsustainable tenancies or unstable communities
- For long-term lettings give priority to categories of need set out in section 167 of HA 1996 (as amended).

RSLs should also:
- Have policies covering transfers and exchanges and give reasonable priority to transfers
- Participate in national and local mobility schemes (this applies to all RSLs other than very small ones)
- Where requested, co-operate with and assist local authorities in fulfilling homelessness duties (HA 1996, s. 213), and in housing those on the statutory register (HA 1996, s. 170)
- Offer at least 50 per cent of vacancies and relets to local authority nominees.

In addition to these performance standards, RSLs must also comply with the relevant tenants' guarantees, the CRE's *Code*

of Practice and any other statutory and Corporation requirements when selecting tenants and allocating homes.

Access routes in practice

Nominations

Most local authorities have written agreements with RSLs
operating in their area specifying the proportion of vacancies
of different types to be set aside for nominees and operational
procedures to be followed. The Housing Corporation's expectation that associations will make available at least 50 per cent
of lettings sets the norm. Nevertheless, higher figures often
apply in instances such as initial lets of properties developed
with local authority assistance, or in relation to family size
housing in areas of housing stress such as Greater London.

Nomination procedures can be divided into three
categories:
1. *Direct nominations:* a single nominee is put forward for
   a specific vacancy.
2. *Non-prioritised pool nominations:* two or more nominees
   are put forward at a time, with the receiving RSL
   determining which will get priority.
3. *Prioritised pool nominations:* two or more nominees are
   put forward at a time, with the order of priority
   predetermined by the nominating local authority.

Nomination agreements generally specify the range of
legitimate reasons for which nominees may be refused by the
receiving RSL. This could, for example, include cases where,
under the RSL's allocations policy, the applicant was not
judged to be in severe housing need, or required a property
of a different size from that available.

Direct applications

In most parts of the country, the majority of RSLs have their
own housing registers or 'waiting lists', although in an

increasing number of areas RSLs are now participating in common housing registers with other social landlords (see p. 42 below). In London, however, this is uncommon. Those allocated RSL tenancies from such waiting lists are referred to as 'direct applicants'. Within broad guidelines as to their underlying responsibilities to meet housing needs and to operate in a fair and equitable manner, RSLs are under no particular legal or regulatory obligations in terms of how they manage their own waiting lists. There is, for example, no requirement to adhere to the 'qualifying persons' rules which apply to local authorities (see pp. 20 *et seq* above).

Some RSLs use waiting lists to promote access to particular types of property (e.g. bedsits) or parts of the housing stock (e.g. blocks or areas considered otherwise 'difficult to let'). In some cases, lists are 'opened' and 'closed' to regulate demand. One RSL, which is developing a telephone-based customer call centre, replaced its application form and waiting list with a telephone administered questionnaire which enables callers to get an instant response on whether their application can be accepted and the sort of property they can expect.

Referrals

In certain areas, particularly London, a significant proportion of those housed by RSLs are referred by voluntary agencies or by statutory bodies other than local authority housing departments. These are generally referred to as 'referrals' (as distinct from 'nominees'). Those rehoused under referral arrangements often have support needs of one kind or another. In some cases, the referring organisation makes a commitment to provide such support, following rehousing. RSLs often agree annual quotas with organisations such as the probation service, or with voluntary bodies which offer housing advice or temporary accommodation to members of minority groups (e.g. ethnic minorities).

Rights to information on part of social housing applicants

Local authority obligations

Local authorities' duties to supply information relating to entries made on the housing register, or rejections of applications, are set out above (see pp. 28–32 above).

A person on the housing register is entitled to see the entry relating to him- or herself and receive a copy free of charge. In common with any other member of the public, applicants are also entitled to be provided with a summary of the authority's allocation scheme. Under section 166 of HA 1996, applicants are also to be provided with 'general information' which will enable them to assess how long it will be before a suitable tenancy becomes available. The *Code of Guidance* states that authorities are not required to provide an estimated waiting time, although they may do so: 'At a minimum, [the authority] should give an applicant an indication of his/her position in the queue and of the likely supply of appropriate properties over the coming year' (draft revised *Code of Practice*, para. 4.19).

In practice, local authority procedures on the provision of this sort of information vary widely. In some cases, leaflets specify points levels at which applicants are generally housed in particular areas or accommodation types, so that these can be used as a benchmark against which to set known points tallies. Providing customised advice about rehousing prospects is clearly simpler under systems with a prominent 'date order' component and, more generally, for authorities with more sophisticated computer systems. However, there can often be communication difficulties where the geographical areas used by the landlord to map rehousing prospects do not correspond with the mental maps of applicants.

Disclosure that a person is on the register, and the information about him or her included in the register, must not be divulged to any other member of the public (s. 166(2)).

The draft revised *Code of Guidance* suggests that this does not preclude disclosure to housing officers, doctors, social workers or RSLs' staff, 'although authorities will wish to preserve confidentiality and supply information only on a "need to know" basis' (para. 4.17).

RSLs' obligations

RSLs are expected to have written lettings policies which are consistent with their governing instruments. Applicants for RSL housing have a right to see these policies. Under the Data Protection Act 1984 (shortly to be replaced by the Data Protection Act 1998), applicants also have the right to see any information held about themselves on computer, together with any other personal information held by the landlord (unless it was given to the landlord, in confidence, by a third party).

In the housing association sector, applicants have no specific right to information on how long it might take for a suitable tenancy to become available. Nevertheless, many RSLs recognise that the provision of such information is good practice because it enables applicants to make informed choices about areas or property types. This makes it possible to 'trade off' the speed with which an applicant may be rehoused against his or her ideal preferences. In practice, it is fairly common for associations to routinely provide information of this sort at the point of application.

Common housing registers

Principles

In many parts of the country, local authorities have joined forces with RSLs to set up common housing registers (CHRs). Fundamentally, all CHRs involve a common database in which all housing applications are stored, and to which all participating landlords have access. Generally, a common application form is used by all participants. From the applicant's point of view, such arrangements have the advantage that they provide a 'one stop shop' for all the social housing in an area, doing away with the need for multiple applications. From the landlords' point of view, CHRs offer the possibility of introducing greater consistency into the allocation of homes, and the elimination of duplication of effort involved in managing separate registers.

CHRs are particularly common in areas where all the local authority housing stock has been transferred to RSLs. Local authorities are permitted to include the statutory register within a CHR under section 162 of HA 1996, though they are obliged to ensure that the housing register entries remain identifiable.

The principle of CHRs is that all applicants in housing need within a given area should have access to social housing through a single channel. This implies that all lettings in the area (including those to existing tenants transferring within social housing) will involve applicants drawn from the CHR. In practice, however, some CHRs are slightly less than comprehensive, with some landlords retaining free-standing waiting lists for certain housing schemes (e.g. property considered 'difficult to let'). There are considerable variations between registers such as in relation to whether transfer applications, sheltered housing or special needs schemes are included.

Types of CHR

The term 'CHR' applies to a variety of types of arrangements. One specific form of CHR involves the participating landlords agreeing on their rehousing criteria so that a common allocations policy (CAP) prevails. Although CAPs exist in a number of areas across the country, the Housing Corporation encourages RSLs to follow independent allocations policies. In practice, where RSLs and local authorities have compared points schemes there have often been few significant policy differences; however, it remains the case that in areas with CAPs it is possible that some applicants will be excluded by all local social landlords.

Most CHRs, however, do not involve CAPs. Collaboration is strictly administrative, rather than at a policy level. In some cases, a sophisticated computerised database and IT network allows all participating landlords to access the register remotely, with the facility to rank the list according to the rehousing priorities of each participant. In other cases, free-standing registers are run by a central agency (often the local authority) with other participating landlords communicating with the administrative centre only by post and telephone or fax. Computer packages can be used to extract lists of applicants to meet the differing priorities of participating landlords; for example, local authorities may exclude applicants who do not meet local residence requirements, while some RSLs can consider all applicants on a needs basis, and others may select those who meet their charitable purposes.

CHRs and nominations

The operation of CHRs calls into question the differentiation of applicants according to their 'source of referral' (e.g. local authority nominee, direct applicant). While there have been claims that CHRs can avoid the bureaucracy of nominations, in most cases local authorities continue to specify which applicants they are nominating and, for statistical purposes (e.g. CORE returns), RSLs are advised to distinguish between these categories according to whether the applicable rehousing prioritisation criteria were those of the local authority (nominees) or the RSL itself (direct applicants). (See under 'Comprehensiveness' in Table 2.)

Summary

Partly as a response to the growing problem of difficult-to-let housing, social landlords are increasingly attempting to market their properties to prospective tenants. Many also advise and assist potential housing applicants at the application stage.

Table 2. Typology of common housing registers

Criteria	Option 1	Option 2	Option 3	Option 4
1. Control				
Who runs register?	LA run register	HA run register	Agency run register	—
Extent of partnership	Equal partnership LA, all RSLs	LA led register	Varying levels of RSL participation possible	—
Control arrangements	Member level policy group	Officer level policy group	Other governing body	No governing body
Marketing image of CHR	Clearly LA led	Area-based but not clearly LA led	Clear partnership	RSL led
Costs	Development costs (IT, staff, other)	Maintenance costs (fixed, variable)	Compensatory savings	—
Cost apportionment	Development LA/RSLs	Maintenance LA/RSLs	—	—
2. Comprehensiveness				
Extent of common arrangements	Application clearing house	CHR	CAP	—
Demand groups included	All applications LA and RSL special needs	LA and RSL nominations only sheltered	Excludes RSL transfers only private tenants	Excludes all transfers, LCHO, shared ownership

Table 2—contd

2.—contd

Property allocated through CHR	All LA and RSL lettings special needs	LA and RSL nominations only sheltered	All except HA transfers, private tenants	LCHO/shared ownership
How do RSL partners allocate?	CHR only	CHR plus transfers	CHR plus transfers plus referrals	CHR plus transfers plus own waiting list
RSL own lettings (i.e. not nominations)	CHR single points order list	CHR multiple points lists	Apply own policies to CHR list outside CHR	—
Nominations	Retain separate agreements with LA identifying nominees	RSLs select from computer list in LA priority order	RSLs select from computer on common points scheme	RSLs select from computer flexibly within lettings plan
3. Information base IT system	Existing LA system	Off-the-shelf purchase	Tailor made	—
IT access	LA only—RSLs use paper forms	LA and all partner RSLs	LA and large partner RSLs	None
Method of communication	Paper/phone only	Fax/e-mail	Telephone line link	Modem link
Monitoring	Monthly returns by RSLs	Management reports from computer system	Sample case monitoring by LA/ CHR manager	—

Table 2—*contd*

4. Application form				
Common application form	Yes	No	—	—
Standard set of data items	JAWs standard	Other standard	Some variations	—
Application forms returned to	Any partner	LA only	—	—
Data input by	Any partner	LA only	Lead agency for demand group	Central bureau
5. Home visits				
Home visits when	Application recorded	Applicant near to offer level	—	—
Home visits by	Partner doing letting	Partner receiving application	LA or central agency only	RSLs only
6. Customer response				
Types of customer information	General booklet	Rehousing chances	Types of property/options	On-line access
Customer choice	Ability to opt out of certain landlords/tenancy types	Number of reasonable offers	Area choice/mobility	—
Access points	LA only	LA and all participating RSLs	LA and some participating RSLs	LA, RSLs and other agencies

Source: Mullins and Niner (1996)

The local authority housing register, for which there is a requirement under HA 1996, has a central role in mediating access to most social housing. Local authorities are subject to a wide-ranging set of legal requirements which determine which applications may be entered on the register and how the system should be managed. Whilst the rights of certain categories of applicants (e.g. homeless households) are protected in law, authorities also have considerable discretion to exclude specific groups from being entered on the register, hence debarring them from access to social housing.

The stipulations governing the housing register also impact on access to RSL tenancies involving nominations from local authorities. In general, the allocation of RSL housing is subject to regulations issued by the Housing Corporation.

Partly to combat problems of fragmentation resulting from stock transfer, many social landlords are looking to set up common housing registers to facilitate access to all social sector tenancies in a given area. Other advantages of CHRs include the potential benefit of a one-stop-shop for applicants, together with a reduction in bureaucracy associated with nominations, and the promotion of moves between local authorities and RSLs and vice versa.

Further reading

Britain, A. and Yanetta, A. (1997). *Housing Allocations in Scotland: A Practice Note.* Edinburgh: Chartered Institute of Housing in Scotland.

Chartered Institute of Housing (1998). *Rehousing Sex Offenders: A Summary of the Legal and Operational Issues.* CIH.

Dean, J., Goodlad, R. and Rosengard, A. (1996). *Models of Practice in Housing Advice.* London: The Stationery Office.

Department of the Environment, Transport and the Regions (2000). *Code of Guidance on the Allocation of Accommodation and Homelessness.* London: Stationery Office.

Grant, C. (1996). *Housing Advice Services: A Good Practice Guide*. Coventry: CIH.

Griffiths, M., Parker, J., Smith, R. and Stirling, T. (1997). *Local Authority Housing Allocations: Systems, Policies and Procedures*. London: DETR.

Henderson, J. (2000). *Children and Housing*. London: Lemos and Crane, Arden's Housing Library.

Housing Corporation (1997). *Performance Standards and Regulatory Guidance for Registered Social Landlords, Third Edition incorporating statutory management guidance under s36 of Housing Act 1996*. London: Housing Corporation.

Mullins, D. and Niner, P. (1996). *Common Housing Registers: An Evaluation and Analysis of Current Practice*. London: Housing Corporation.

Niner, P. (1997). *The Early Impact of the Housing Act 1996 and Housing Benefit Changes*. London: Shelter.

Parker, J., Smith, R. and Williams, P. (1992). *Access, Allocations and Nominations: The Role of Housing Associations*. London: HMSO.

Parker, J. and Stirling, T. (1995). *Seen To Be Fair: A Guide to Allocating Rented Housing*. Cardiff: Housing Management Advisory Panel for Wales.

Pawson, H., Kearns, A., Keoghan, M., Malcolm, J. and Morgan, J. (1997). *Managing Voids and Difficult to Let Property*. London: Housing Corporation.

Prescott-Clarke, P., Clemens, S. and Park, A. (1994). *Routes into Local Authority Housing: A Study of Local Authority Waiting Lists and New Tenancies*. London: HMSO.

Yanetta, A., Third, H. and Pawson, H. (1997). *Nomination Arrangements in Scotland*. Edinburgh: Scottish Office Central Research Unit.

3.
Mobility within Social Housing

Overall framework / Transfer eligibility / Inter-area
moves / Contractual succession / Landlord's
interest moves / Other urgent or exceptional moves
within social housing

Chapter 2 describes the framework governing access to social
housing for new tenants of local authorities and RSLs. Social
housing allocations also involve transfers or exchanges of
existing tenants. In total, lettings of this sort account for over
a third of all social sector lettings.

Moves within social housing take a variety of forms. A
basic distinction can be made between the great majority
which are tenant-instigated and those where the motivation
for the move is the landlord's own interest. Drawing on this
distinction, this chapter describes the various types of intra-
social housing moves and details the relevant legislation and
regulatory guidance which governs these. It also covers social
landlords' policies and practices in managing transfers, exchanges and other mobility options.

Overall framework

Moves by existing social rented sector tenants are specifically
excluded from Part VI of HA 1996. Although the Act obliges
local authorities to integrate their assessment of all qualifying

persons (e.g. homeless households and other new applicants), this requirement does *not* extend to those who are already tenants of councils or RSLs. Similarly, the following categories of lettings are also outside the remit of Part VI:

- Statutory succession (e.g. a widow succeeding to a tenancy on her husband's death)
- Assignment (e.g. mutual exchanges)
- Transfers of secure or introductory tenancies under the provisions of the matrimonial and related domestic legislation
- Becoming a secure tenant after an introductory tenancy
- Successions or assignments involving introductory tenancies.

This is achieved by specific exemptions from the application of Part VI under section 160. A common factor of these categories is that there is no *new* interest in land being created. Rather, such instances involve a *continuation* of a previous interest. In terms of Part VI, such lettings are not classed as 'allocations'.

Additionally, further exemptions have been made by statutory instrument for:

1. secure tenants from Northern Ireland and Scotland;
2. assured tenants of housing associations in Scotland, or landlords who acquired the property from a local authority in Scotland or from Scottish Homes;
3. those entitled to rehousing under section 39 of the Land Compensation Act 1973 (see p. 35 above); and
4. those who are granted tenancies following repurchase under legislation designed to assist those who have bought defective housing.

Although Part VI does not apply, as discussed below, certain sorts of intra-social housing moves are subject to other statutes or to case-law. This applies, in particular, to moves of the 'landlord's interest' rather than to tenant-instigated type. Case-law is also relevant to restrictions on eligibility for transfers.

Succession and assignment are dealt with only briefly in this chapter, since these are more fully covered in another publication in this series; see C. Hunter, *Tenants' Rights* (1995).

In the case of RSLs, there is a requirement in the *Performance Standards* that 'lettings policies should cover transfers and exchanges and give reasonable priority to transfer applicants (including applicants from other RSLs) where this meets priority housing need, makes best use of stock, or contributes to stable communities' (Standard F2.2).

Compliance with this standard is monitored by comparing levels of transfers between RSLs and making enquiries about outlying levels of performance.

Transfer eligibility

Most social landlords maintain some form of register of existing tenants who have expressed a wish to move, or who the landlord considers require to be moved for management reasons (see pp. 56–58 below). Among local authorities, this list is sometimes integrated with the statutory housing register (see Chap. 2), though individual records need to be distinguishable from those of new applicants. As noted in Chapter 2, entries relating to tenants aspiring to a transfer may also be entered on CHRs in areas where these are established. Indeed, in some areas the lack of local transfer opportunities for tenants of RSLs which had little stock of suitable sizes for their tenants to transfer to in the local authority area was a major stimulus to the development of common registers.

Many landlords apply restrictions on eligibility for transfer list registration. The most common eligibility conditions are:

- No rent arrears
- Some degree of housing need
- Residence in the current property for a given period (e.g. one year)
- No breach of tenancy agreement resulting in service of a notice seeking possession
- No current right-to-buy application.

Some RSLs restrict entry to transfer (and waiting) lists on the grounds of income. In part, this reflects the historic purpose of particular RSLs. Another practice is to make entry to the transfer list conditional on the probability that an applicant will be housed within a given time period, usually a year. Such restrictions are justified on the grounds that they reduce landlords' queue management costs, as well as providing greater certainty to tenants whose applications are accepted.

As far as local authorities are concerned, the implementation of restrictions on transfer eligibility is very much a matter for their own discretion. As they fall outside the constraints of Part VI of HA 1996 (see p. 51 above), any transfer scheme

> 'falls to be assessed not on the basis of the statutory provisions or related ministerial guidance, but in accordance with general principles of public law. That is to say that the court will close its eyes to the statute or the ministerial guidance. Although they do not govern [transfers], their substantive content may have a bearing on the lawfulness of the position at common law.'

(Per Richards J in *R v Islington LBC, ex p Reilly and Mannix* (1998).) So, for example, authorities may not adopt their policies so rigidly as to fetter their discretion in considering the individual circumstances of particular applicants for housing. Thus, there is no reason in principal why rent arrears should not be taken into account in considering a transfer application. However, in *R v Islington LBC, ex p Aldabbagh* (1994), the council's guideline that, in cases of rent arrears, transfers 'should only be agreed if agreement to pay current rent plus a regular contribution to reduce the arrears' was unlawful because it was stated in the form of a rule which allowed no exceptions.

Any scheme must be rational and in *R v Tower Hamlets LBC, ex p Siraj Uddin* (1999) (see the 'Case report' below) Keene J said that it is to be expected that 'any rational transfer scheme would seek to observe' the principle in the *Code of Guidance*

that authorities will generally 'wish to ensure that their allocation schemes give greater preference to the more severe cases
of need', at least where 'other factors, such as the requirements
of the efficient management of the stock, did not militate
against it'.

A rational scheme must take into account the number
of persons in the household affected by a particular problem,
be it overcrowding (*R v Lambeth LBC, ex p Ashley* (1996)) or ill
health (*Siraj Uddin* (1999) (above and below)), and also the
full range of problems (*R v Islington LBC, ex p Reilly and Mannix*
(1998)) to provide a composite assessment of housing need.

> ### Case report
> Under the transfer policy operated by Tower Hamlets
> LBC, transfers on the grounds of ill health were pointed
> within five categories. The categorisation depended
> on whether one or more members of the household
> fell within the particular category. Three households
> who each had more than one member who suffered
> from ill health challenged the council's policy.
>
> In quashing the policy, the judge found that it
> did not allow for a composite assessment. An alloca-
> tions scheme which awards the same number of points
> whether there is one person suffering from ill health
> or three was held to be irrational. The judge continued,
> however: 'That does not mean that an allocations
> scheme has simply to multiply the number of points in
> a given category by the number of persons in the
> household who fall within it. That could give rise to
> anomalies. No doubt some form of sliding scale would
> be more appropriate ...' *R v Tower Hamlets LBC, ex p
> Siraj Uddin* (1999)

This still, however, leaves a wide discretion as to how transfer
policies are operated.

> ### Case report: scope for discretion on transfer eligibility
> An applicant had been on the authority's transfer list
> for 16 years. In 1994, the estate was handed over to a

Housing Action Trust (HAT). The council decided that tenants could remain on the transfer list for so long as the HAT maintained a reciprocal arrangement of accepting council nominees for rehousing. In 1996, the HAT ceased accepting nominations and the council therefore removed the applicant and other former tenants from the transfer list. Tenants were advised that they could apply to join the ordinary scheme for housing allocation, but would be given no extra 'credit' for the time spent on the transfer list. The policy was upheld. *R v Brent LBC, ex p Jerke* (1998)

Inter-area moves

The vast majority of moves within social housing involve tenants transferring to another property owned by the same landlord. For local authorities, and often for RSLs, this restricts movement to a limited geographical area. The national Housing Organisations Mobility and Exchange Scheme (HOMES) exists to enable inter-area, inter-landlord moves. In theory, HOMES nominees need not be existing tenants of the nominating landlord. In practice, however, this is usually the case.

Most local authorities in England and Wales participate in the HOMES scheme and agree to set aside a small quota of lettings for HOMES nominees. Similarly, authorities have a small annual quota of outgoing mobility opportunities. A person wishing to be nominated for a move under the HOMES scheme applies to his or her current social landlord or local authority. Applicants are prioritised for nomination according to specific criteria relating to their 'need to move' as well as according to their housing needs (see Chap. 4). Under these special criteria, priority might be assigned according to e.g. an applicant's need to take up employment in another area or to be closer to relatives or friends to give or receive support. Incoming nominees are also likely to have their housing needs assessed by the 'receiving landlord' to determine their rehousing priority and the size and type of accommodation considered appropriate on the basis of local policies.

Contractual succession

Secure and assured tenants have statutory rights of succession under HA 1985. These are described in full in C. Hunter, *Tenants' Rights* (1995). In addition, under the terms of the tenancy agreement, some social landlords make a contractual commitment to extend these rights. It is not uncommon, for example, for landlords to accord the right to succeed to same-sex partners who are not covered by the Act. In such cases, there is a technical requirement for the tenancy application to be entered on the statutory housing register. This is because the applicant is not an existing tenant or a person with a *statutory* right to succeed and, therefore, is not excluded from the scope of Part VI of HA 1996.

Landlord's interest moves

In general, moves within social housing are prioritised according to housing need. RSLs are subject to explicit Housing Corporation regulatory guidance on this point. As a rule, tenants' present circumstances are judged against similar criteria to those applied to housing register applicants. Issues such as overcrowding, medical needs or property unsuitability are important (see Chap. 4). In addition, waiting time is sometimes considered. There is evidence that this factor tends to be taken into account more commonly for transfers than for housing register applicants.

Nevertheless, a significant proportion of intra-social housing moves come about as a result of the landlord's management interest. Examples of such moves include tenants 'decanted' to permit major works or demolition, and moves to facilitate better use of the housing stock. Making better use of stock can involve prioritising, for example, applicants currently living in supported or adapted housing who no longer require the support or adaptations provided, or tenants currently underoccupying their home and prepared to move to a smaller dwelling. Explicit reference is made to these categories in Housing Corporation regulatory guidance for RSLs.

Decants

Local authorities

Where tenants do not agree to move, authorities can only oblige them to move by taking possession proceedings. Two grounds for possession are available under Schedule 2 to HA 1985. The first is Ground 10 where the *landlord* intends to carry out works of demolition or reconstruction and possession is necessary for that purpose. The second is Ground 10A where it is intended to dispose of the property for redevelopment by the private sector. In both cases, suitable alternative accommodation must be made available.

RSLs

The situation differs for RSLs, depending on whether the tenants are secure or assured. If secure, then the same grounds for possession apply as for local authorities. If assured, then it may be possible to rely on Ground 6 of Schedule 2 to HA 1988. Alternatively, the landlord may wish to offer suitable alternative accommodation and rely on the discretionary Ground 9.

Underoccupation

Many social landlords place a high priority on minimising underoccupation in their housing stock and the importance of this issue has been emphasised by central government for some time. A common means of achieving this is to accord rehousing priority to existing tenants on the grounds that their current home is larger than their requirements. With increasing pressure on social housing in some areas of the country, many landlords have increased the priority weighting for under-occupation over the past few years.

In addition, social landlords commonly provide other incentives for underoccupiers to move to smaller homes. These include meeting removal expenses and providing extra cash payments. Such payments now have a statutory basis under Schedule 18 to HA 1996, although the clause does not restrict their availability to cases of this sort.

Under Ground 16 of Schedule 2 to HA 1985, a local authority may, in certain circumstances, recover possession of an underoccupied dwelling following succession. In a sense, this can be seen as a type of decant move. The rules relate to properties where the 'accommodation provided ... is more extensive than is reasonably required by the tenant' and where the successor is someone other than the deceased tenant's spouse. In this situation, an authority may issue a notice seeking possession between six and twelve months after the death. A court may order possession, depending on whether this is considered reasonable, and whether suitable alternative accommodation is available.

Other urgent or exceptional moves within social housing

As well as decants, most social landlords also recognise a second category of 'transfer' moves which have a particularly high priority and which generally need to be handled outside the main allocations system. These relate to groups regarded as needing to move because their housing or area context is intolerable. Factors involved in such cases include:

- Domestic violence
- Neighbour disputes

- Racial harassment, and
- Acute medical priorities.

The need for 'extra-system' rapid move procedures partly follows from an acceptance that it is impractical for any set of allocations policies to anticipate every problematic circumstance or combination of circumstances which might affect a tenant.

In cases involving domestic violence, the grounds for the move are that it is unreasonable to continue to occupy the home (draft revised *Code of Guidance*, ch. 11). From a legal perspective, and in terms of the *Code*, therefore, housing applications from people experiencing or threatened with domestic violence are viewed as homelessness applications, irrespective of tenure. Persons to whom the local authority owes the two-year minimum rehousing duty under Part VII of HA 1996 qualify to be entered on the housing register (see pp. 86–87 below). From an administrative point of view, however, many local authorities opt to prioritise council tenants via accelerated transfer schemes, often referred to as 'management transfers'.

Racial harassment transfers require sensitivity and urgency in the matching process. While transferring the victims of racial harassment rather than taking action against the perpetrators is rarely the best option (see Seager and Jeffery, *Eliminating Racial Harassment* (1994)), occasions arise where this is necessary for the victims' safety. Many authorities therefore prioritise racial harassment transfers for speedy offers of rehousing. However, it is important that those rehoused under such policies are not penalised by being offered poorer quality or smaller size housing than their existing dwelling. Care is also required to ensure that rehousing does not result in the risk of further harassment. Thus, harassment transfers may be one of the few cases where it is appropriate to relax the normal process of matching an applicant to a property.

There are obviously dangers of proliferation and abuse of extra-system procedures if these become recognised as the principal means of securing a better outcome for applicants in the context of shortages. Medical assessment procedures have been critically examined in this respect. For example, in a formal investigation of race and council housing in Hackney, the CRE found evidence that the medical assessment system was being used as a 'bargaining counter' since 'it is difficult to accept that such a high proportion of people actually had such significant medical problems'. Moreover, white applicants were almost twice as likely as black applicants to have file references to medical needs (CRE, 1994, p. 68).

Summary

Moves within social housing account for over a third of all social sector lettings. A basic distinction can be drawn between those where the move is tenant-instigated and those where it is in the landlord's own interest (e.g. decants).

Intra-social housing moves are generally outside the remit of the allocations framework prescribed by HA 1996. Consequently, landlords enjoy much greater discretion for these lettings than in the case of lettings to 'new tenants'.

Subject to limitations deriving from case-law, landlords often impose eligibility criteria on transfer list registration. There are also specific legal requirements which govern decanting.

Most social landlords recognise an 'exceptional' category of 'transfer' moves having a particularly high priority and which are normally dealt with outside the main allocations system. Such arrangements cater for instances such as domestic violence and racial harassment.

Further reading

Barelli, J. (1992). *Underoccupation in Local Authority and Housing Association Housing*. London: HMSO.

Commission for Racial Equality (1984). *Race and Council Housing in Hackney. Report of Formal Investigation*. London, CRE.

Griffiths, M., Parker, J., Smith, R. and Stirling, T. (1997). *Local Authority Housing Allocations: Systems, Policies and Procedures*. London: DETR.

Hunter, C. (1995). *Tenants' Rights*. London: Lemos and Crane, Arden's Housing Library.

Maclennan, D. and Kay, H. (1994). *Moving On, Crossing Divides: A Report on Policies and Procedure for Tenants Transferring in Local Authorities and Housing Associations*. London: HMSO.

Parker, J. and Stirling, T. (1995). *Seen To Be Fair: A Guide to Allocating Rented Housing*. Cardiff: Housing Management Advisory Panel for Wales.

Seager, R. and Jeffrey, J. (1994). *Eliminating Racial Harassment*. London: Lemos Associates.

4.
Social Housing Allocations Schemes: Systems and Objectives

Housing needs and prioritisation of applications /
Allocations systems / Assessing housing needs /
Customer input / Tenant selection and property
matching / Offers and refusals / Appeals
procedures / Local lettings initiatives

In allocating tenancies, social landlords must work within the
established statutory and regulatory framework as described
elsewhere in this guide (see especially Chaps 2, 5 and 6). For
local authorities, much of this framework is set out in HA 1996.
For RSLs, the Housing Corporation's *Performance Standards*
are also important. Nevertheless, landlords retain a large
measure of discretion in discharging their allocations function.
Local authorities, for example, are obliged to accord 'reasonable preference' to a number of specified groups of applicants
(see Chap. 5). Other than that, however, they remain largely
free to select their own system for prioritising applications,
including the choice of indicators of housing needs and the
relative weighting of these.

This chapter discusses the rationale for prioritising
allocations and the various ways in which applicants' housing

needs are measured. It goes on to describe the different types of allocations systems operated by social landlords in practice and looks at some of the practicalities involved in matching applicants to properties. Finally, it examines the ways that some landlords vary or adapt their allocations systems to address problems of unpopular or difficult-to-let housing and to promote balanced communities. The chapter covers matters which apply to both local authorities and RSLs. Issues specific to one or other sector, mainly for legal reasons, are discussed in Chapters 5 and 6.

Housing needs and prioritisation of applications

In general, social landlords are expected to prioritise housing allocations according to applicants' assessed housing needs. This has been the main thrust of central government advice for many years and is reflected in the dynamics of most social landlords' allocations systems. By and large, therefore, re-housing lists are ranked on the basis of some combination of urgency of, severity of and duration of need.

However, it is accepted that there are instances where factors other than housing need should be taken into account in determining rehousing priority. The Housing Corporation's *Performance Standards*, for example, explicitly define the circumstances in which it is legitimate for an RSL to depart from this principle. These can be summarised as cases where:

• Such allocations would make better use of the housing stock
• Flexibility would promote the letting of unpopular or difficult-to-let housing
• The landlord is seeking to improve community balance in a particular locality.

Examples of instances where prioritisation might be justified on the grounds of better use of the housing stock include existing tenants underoccupying their present home and those needing to be decanted to make way for demolition, refurbishment or sale (see p. 57 above). The factors involved in tailoring allocations systems to address unpopular housing and in pursuing community lettings policies are described in more detail later in this chapter.

Allocations systems

The allocations system is the way that landlords form up rehousing applications into a queue or set of queues which reflect the landlord's objectives and priorities. Designing an allocations system involves two sets of decisions on the part of the landlord:

1. What degree of priority should be given to different categories of applicant (e.g. mainstream transfer cases, community care cases)?
2. Should each category of applicant be assessed in the same way?

Allocations systems in social housing are often categorised under one or more of the following four general headings:

1. *Points or categories of need systems:* scores are given for different needs factors and then aggregated to give a total number of points or a needs score.
2. *Date order systems:* rehousing offers are made according to the date order of applications made.
3. *'Merit' systems:* each applicant is subjectively assessed on his or her particular housing circumstances.
4. *Targets or quotas for different access channels or groups:* applicants are categorised according to their access route (e.g. decants, management transfers) or their status (e.g. elderly, ethnic minority) and the proportion of lettings to applicants in each channel group is set by a quota or target.

In practice, however, the precise allocations rules, systems and procedures operated by different landlords are extremely varied and, in many cases, systems include elements of two or more of the ideal types listed above. For example, waiting time may be one of many elements reflected in a points allocation under a points system. Similarly, different approaches to prioritisation may be applied to different categories of applicant. Transfer cases, for instance, may be ranked by date order, whilst other groups are prioritised strictly according to their current recorded circumstances in terms of housing needs. Targets may be used as a monitoring device rather than as an allocation mechanism (see Chapter 8 for a discussion of the differences between targets and quotas).

Whatever a landlord's decisions about the rules and mechanics of its allocations system, both local authorities and RSLs are obliged to publish summary details of the scheme to be available to tenants and other members of the public on request (HA 1996, s. 168; Performance Standard G3.1). Local authorities are also required to make available a full manual which sets out the details of their scheme for inspection and sale.

Assessing housing needs

Providing that they accord 'reasonable preference' to applicants falling within seven specified groups (see Chap. 5), social landlords may define their own criteria for the measurement and weighting of housing needs. Eight general categories of need criteria may be identified, though not all of these are included in every prioritisation scheme:

- Insecurity of tenure
- Lacking or sharing facilities (e.g. kitchen, bathroom, WC)
- Disrepair
- Suitability of property with respect to applicant's needs (e.g. overcrowding)
- Medical needs
- Social needs (e.g. harassment, employment location)

- Housing costs (i.e. need to move to more affordable housing)
- Waiting time (and residence).

Exactly how each type of need is assessed, and the relative weightings accorded to each, are matters for individual landlords. The treatment of waiting time tends to be particularly contentious. Because of its simplicity, including waiting time as a prioritisation criterion often appeals to applicants and tenants. At the same time, however, such a system may be criticised as rewarding those who are able to wait (perhaps because their housing circumstances are not especially unsatisfactory). A compromise position is to treat waiting time as relevant only in the prioritisation of pairs (or larger numbers) of cases where all other relevant factors are equal.

Where waiting time is interpreted as 'time in need', it may be justified in terms of a recognition that an applicant's ability to cope with poor housing conditions will reduce over time. The rate with which time in need points are accrued may depend on the assessed severity of need involved.

In general, rehousing prioritisation is based on information provided by the applicant on a standard application form. The details entered by the applicant are also the basis for determining the appropriate property size, type and area given the household's characteristics, and the applicant's preferences. Sometimes forms are completed with the help of a housing officer who can interpret the questions and responses and, if necessary, provide advice to inform choices (see below). In some cases the application involves a home visit by a housing officer to verify some detail of the application (e.g. in relation to the property's condition or features).

Home visits may be particularly important for applicants with care or support needs, since such applications are often likely to involve claims that existing properties are unsuitable. Claims of this sort require verification. All applications where ill health or disability may be a relevant issue generally involve input from specialist health professionals, occupational therapists or social workers. This may relate to the assessment of the applicant's condition, to the suitability of his or her current accommodation, or to the features of the property needed. In some local authorities, decisions on cases of this sort are routinely informed (or determined) by advice from a medical adviser employed by the local health authority.

Customer input

On the whole, social housing is allocated according to rules and procedures and in the light of the applicant's assessed rehousing priority and needs. In most cases, for example, the size of a property for which an applicant is considered eligible will be determined by a clear set of 'matching criteria'. The possibility of opting to pay a higher rent for a larger property is generally not on offer. Under most allocations policies there is, however, some scope for customer input in determining which vacancies are considered suitable by the landlord. Most commonly, this relates to locational preferences.

Applicants are usually offered the opportunity to state in which area(s) they prefer to be rehoused. In some cases, such choices are highly constrained by a requirement that, for example, an applicant choose at least four of ten possible areas. Choice may also be constrained by an administrative decision on the landlord's part to divide the area of operation into very large sub-areas. On the other hand, some landlords permit applicants to make highly specific area preferences, right down to street level. Similarly, some landlords allow specific preferences on property type and/or facilities.

In any system involving applicants' area preferences it is implicit that rehousing queues for each administrative area are held separately, so that the greater the demand and the smaller the area, the longer the applicant is likely to need to wait, all other things being equal. Consequently, there is a trade-off for applicants between ideal area and waiting time. Explaining such implications may be an important function of the initial application interview and is often important from the landlord's point of view because it provides an opportunity to encourage applicants to consider less popular areas where vacancies may be more numerous.

The fact that applicants are allowed to state a locational preference does not necessarily mean that this will be respected by the landlord when it comes to making a tenancy offer. Moreover, there may be considerable scope for misunderstanding if the administrative areas used for recording area preferences do not coincide with applicants' 'mental maps'. Offers which may be regarded as 'in the applicants' area of preference' by the landlord may be outside of the area which the applicant had intended to or would have specified had the categories allowed this. Offers in unwanted areas are less likely to be accepted by applicants and in some cases landlords treat such refusals as legitimate so that the offer may be disregarded for the purposes of any specified limit (see below). Particularly in local authorities, there is also the possibility that area preference may be regarded as sacrosanct for one group (e.g. transfer applicants) and merely advisory for another (e.g. homeless households).

Another option sometimes allowed to applicants for local authority housing is whether an RSL tenancy (through a nomination) would be considered. Again, expressed preferences here will not necessarily be treated as inviolate. There are considerable variations in the quality of information provided by local authorities to inform such decisions. Some authorities provide booklets with basic information about each RSL operating in the area, including numbers, types and locations of properties and rent levels. Some allow applicants to specify any RSLs which they do not wish to be considered for.

Tenant selection and property matching

Parties to allocation decisions

In most cases social landlords' decisions on matching vacancies with applicants are made by paid officials, often aided by computer programmes drawing on databases of applicant and property details. Under government regulations (S.I. 1997 No. 483 (England) and S.I. 1997 No. 45 (Wales)), elected local authority members are prohibited from involvement in the decision-making process where either the dwelling concerned is in the member's ward, or the person concerned lives in the member's ward. (See also *R v Port Talbot BC, ex p Jones* (pp. 85–86 below), which is an example of improper interference by councillors.) These rules do not, however, compromise members' responsibilities for determining overall local authority allocations policies and for monitoring their implementation. Neither do they impede members in seeking or providing information on behalf of applicants who are their constituents.

A few landlords have experimented with involving tenants in allocation decisions in particular circumstances such as local lettings schemes. Tenant involvement is sometimes, though not always, a feature of community lettings initiatives (see p. 76 below). Arrangements of this sort need to be set up with extreme care to avoid the possibility that they will result in unfair or unlawful discrimination. With this in mind, one approach has been to allow community representatives to determine only the appropriate type of household for each vacancy as it arises, rather than selecting the actual individual to be offered each tenancy. Another tack has been to allow community representatives to comment on proposed allocations, with no obligation on the part of the landlord to act on any comments put forward. This raises particular difficulties as to passing on of confidential information (see pp. 41–42 above) and the appropriateness, in any event, of sharing personal information on applicants in this way.

Matching process

The matching process used by social landlords generally involves two distinct elements:

1. a broad brush matching of households to property, on the basis of largely objective factors, and

2. a fine-tuning, taking into account other relevant circumstances involving more subjective judgements on the
part of the officials concerned.

'Broad brush' matching is intended to produce a shortlist of
applicants potentially suitable for a specific vacancy. Factors
taken account at this stage would include, for example, the
applicant's priority, the property's size, and any other special
requirements or preferences on the applicant's part (in relation
to e.g. the floor level or property location). In making decisions
about property size requirements, landlords refer to information on the number of bedrooms to which the household
is entitled under the landlord's standard matching criteria as
laid out in its allocations policy. In some cases, policies contain
additional restrictions such as limits on the storey height of
flats to be offered to families with young children.

The fine-tuning stage is where the shortlist is prioritised
to determine exactly which applicant will be offered the vacancy first. This process is more likely to involve assessments
relating to, for example, the competing claims of different
applicants with a similar rehousing priority, or the extent to
which an applicant will 'fit in' to the surrounding community,
given the known characteristics and/or behaviour of neighbouring tenants.

Sensitive lettings: the case of sex offenders

Where landlords emphasise the importance of assessing whether an applicant will 'fit in' with his or her neighbours, this
is generally known as a 'sensitive lettings' approach. Given
that it considers the impact of a potential tenant on his or her
surroundings, this strategy is akin to a 'community lettings'
approach (see p. 76 below). One group for whom this approach
is often seen as essential is sex offenders. As noted in Chapter
3, good practice guidance generally advises against excluding
them from eligibility for rehousing. In determining where a
sex offender should be rehoused, a risk assessment should be
carried out. This will consider a number of factors including:

1. The appropriateness of the area in terms of proximity to schools and the local child density (bearing in mind that there is no such thing as a child-free neighbourhood).
2. The appropriateness of the stock: blocks with concierges and/or CCTV are often considered particularly suitable, but where such 'solutions' begin to lead to 'bunching' of offenders they are not sustainable. Flatted accommodation in child-free blocks is favoured by some landlords.
3. The proposed support package to be offered by appropriate agencies (e.g. Social Services, the Probation Service).

Dealing with sex offenders also raises important questions about information management. On the one hand, it is essential that appropriate information about an applicant who is a sex offender is shared between agencies. Protocols to regulate such disclosures are recommended in good practice guidance. Within a landlord organisation, on the other hand, there is a need to restrict the disclosure of information about an applicant's background to those who need to know. There are, for example, differing views on whether this should generally include the estate manager responsible for a block where a sex offender has been rehoused. One argument against informing staff at this level is the increased risk of wider disclosure (e.g. to tenants) to which this might give rise.

Offers and refusals

One of the most distinctive characteristics of most social housing allocation processes is the way in which applicants are presented with one offer of a property at a time with a very short period to decide whether to accept or refuse it. This experience may be contrasted with search procedures for private rented tenancies or house purchase where the user typically draws up a shortlist of possible options and makes a decision between several options at the same time. The lack of choice available to most social housing applicants is exacerbated by the consequences of refusing reasonable offers.

This is because many social landlords limit the number of tenancy offers made to applicants and apply sanctions where an applicant reaches the end of his or her quota. Commonly, limits are one, two or three offers. This is motivated, in part, by the need to maximise the proportion of offers which are accepted, so reducing rent loss owing to dwellings standing empty awaiting letting. Sometimes the limits vary according to the applicant's access route, so that the limit for transfer applicants might be more generous than for others.

Given the significance of offers limits, it is important to define exactly what constitutes an 'offer'. There is no statutory definition. In practice, most offers are made or confirmed in writing. Nevertheless, it is not unusual for applicants to be contacted informally in advance of, or instead of, being sent a formal offer letter. This is particularly common in the case of difficult-to-let properties where allocators believe that there might be a need for some negotiation or reassurance. For monitoring purposes, RSLs are advised that 'a "tenancy offer" is defined as any offer recorded on the landlord's internal information systems or on the property file. In this sense, "offers" may include "verbal offers" as well as written offers provided that they are recorded in this way' (NHF CORE manual).

Some landlords routinely withdraw offers considered to have been unreasonable. This can happen where it is discovered that an offer has been made on the basis of inaccurate information about, for example, the household's needs or the property's characteristics. On the other hand, an offer matching the landlord's adopted standards and other policies is normally seen as reasonable even if the applicant is not happy with it. Whether an unwanted offer is 'reasonable' is often the subject of appeals (see below).

The sanction usually applied to applicants exceeding their quota of offers is to suspend their application for a given period, often one year. Alternatively, part of the applicant's points total may be removed. In some cases even harsher penalties, such as cancellation of the application, may be applied. In dealing with such cases, local authorities must (as in all their activities) apply the principles of administrative law (*R v Westminster City Council, ex p Nadhum Husain* (1998); see p. 31 above).

Appeals procedures

In this context, an appeal may be defined as 'an opportunity to ask for a review of one of more aspects of the decisions relating to the application'; this may be distinguished from a complaint, which is 'a stated dissatisfaction by a service user with the process followed in their case' (definitions from Britain and Yanetta (1997)). In practice, however, the concepts of appeals and complaints are closely related, and an appeal against a decision may also involve a complaint about how it was reached.

As noted above, the reasonableness of offers is a common subject of appeals. Other matters often raised include disagreement about housing needs assessment and, in local authorities, about exclusions from the housing register (see Chap. 2). Appeals on this latter issue are subject to statutory guidance (HA 1996, s. 164(5)), as are appeals against offers made in discharge of an authority's duty to secure accommodation under Part VII of HA 1996 (homelessness). There is, however, no statutory framework for appeals on other matters.

In practice, local authority appeals mechanisms generally involve a two-stage process, with the matter first being considered by the officer responsible for allocations. In cases where the appellant remains unhappy, there is sometimes a procedure allowing the question to be considered by more senior officers such as the Director of Housing. Good practice advice suggests that where an appeal is upheld, the issues involved should be analysed so that action can be taken, where possible, to prevent a recurrence of the problem.

Local lettings initiatives

Local lettings schemes are arrangements for allocating homes in specific areas which differ from those generally operated by the landlord in question. Such schemes tend to be motivated by two (often related) concerns, which are to promote:

- Letting unpopular and otherwise difficult-to-let housing, and
- Community balance in social, demographic or economic terms.

Allocating difficult-to-let housing

Local lettings policies designed to improve the speed with which otherwise 'low demand' properties are let are generally geared towards:

- Widening the range of applicants eligible for consideration, and/or
- Generating increased interest among potential tenants through offering various incentives.

Widening the range of potential tenants is likely to involve lowering or removing housing needs thresholds which would otherwise disqualify many people from eligibility for social housing. In association with such measures, or independently, landlords may promote or advertise the availability of tenancies in 'low demand' areas. This may be done through, for example, press advertising or targeted leafleting.

A wide range of incentives are offered by social landlords to encourage interest in low demand properties among potential applicants. These include:

1. relaxing standard property size matching criteria (so that e.g. an applicant normally qualifying for a one-

bedroom flat might be offered a three-bedroom property);

2. enabling applicants to choose between several alternative offers at the same time;
3. introducing larger rent differentials in relation to area popularity;
4. offering decoration allowances or other cash payments; and
5. offering rent-free periods at the start of the tenancy.

Another management technique, particularly commonly implemented in relation to low demand areas, is accompanied viewing. This gives the accompanying housing officer a chance to 'sell' the vacancy in the manner of an estate agent and to reassure the applicant about uncompleted repairs or other concerns. An alternative is the mass lettings or 'estate lettings day' approach adopted by some landlords where many vacancies on a particular estate (or group of neighbouring estates) are offered simultaneously. To maximise flexibility, and to provide an incentive for applicants, normal rules on offer limits (see p. 71 above) are generally suspended in these cases.

The need for RSLs to adopt special arrangements in relation to low demand housing is specifically acknowledged by the Housing Corporation. *Performance Standards* acknowledges that it is permissible for associations to depart from the principle of prioritising rehousing on the basis of housing need where this would 'significantly reduce' the number of empty homes. Local authorities are allowed similar latitude under paragraph 5.18 of the draft revised *Code of Guidance*:

> 'There may be cases where the only way an authority can ensure full use of all vacant stock is by giving some preference to categories of persons whose characteristics are not reflected in the statutory priority categories [see Chap. 5]. For example, some authorities adopt special strategies on hard-to-let property, granting tenancies to whoever is willing to take the property, provided that there is no other way of letting the property and that the property is not suitable to

meet the needs of persons or households falling within
the statutory priority categories.'

Community lettings

The term 'community lettings' describes 'allocations policies
which ... take account of the potential tenant's contribution
to that community in which the vacancy has occurred'
(Griffiths *et al.*, 1996, p. 1). The aim is to use the allocations
system to engineer a specific social, demographic or economic
mix within the population of an estate or neighbourhood.

Community lettings policies are inspired by the general
belief that social problems are compounded by concentrations
of deprived residents and that community balance is a concept
which can be operationalised within an allocations policy.
Three other assumptions which, to varying degrees, often
underlie community lettings approaches are that:

1. high child density results in vandalism and anti-social
   behaviour and should be avoided;
2. community benefits accrue from giving preference to
   local people when vacancies occur; and
3. it is practical, legitimate and beneficial to exclude
   applicants who might engage in anti-social behaviour.

Community lettings approaches are sometimes applied
to newly built estates to forestall potential social problems
which might arise in the future. More often, however, they
are attempted in areas of low demand housing affected by
social problems such as crime or delinquency. The objective
in such cases is partly to 'break the cycle' through which an
area's negative image reinforces and is reinforced by the
characteristics of the people housed in the area. If successful,
it is hoped that, over time, this will enhance residential stability. Lower tenancy turnover will reduce void rates. In the short
term, however, such policies may imply *higher* void rates, since
some potential applicants will be screened out (see below).

Generally, a community lettings policy involves an
explicit departure from the principle of prioritising rehousing

solely on the basis of housing need. In the RSL sector, as noted above, there is a general authorisation, on the part of the Housing Corporation, for associations to allocate on grounds other than housing need where this involves difficult-to-let housing.

> **Example: regulation of community lettings policies**
>
> In the application of community lettings schemes in circumstances other than difficult-to-let housing (e.g. newly built estates), the Housing Corporation sets out a number of conditions which must be met. These are that the policy:
>
> 1. is exceptional and has been approved by the relevant local authority and the RSL's governing body;
> 2. clearly defines the area/set of homes to which it applies;
> 3. has defined objectives aimed at preventing or tackling social problems in that area which can be demonstrated to exist;
> 4. is part of a strategy for tackling these problems which involves a revised approach to housing management or the physical aspects of the homes involved, or both;
> 5. will not last for more than three years unless the Corporation agrees to its extension;
> 6. includes arrangements for monitoring and reporting on progress in relation to the scheme's objectives; and
> 7. has been sent to the relevant regional office of the Corporation.
>
> Similarly for the local authority sector, the *Code of Guidance* allows that allocations policies 'could (legitimately) extend to selecting tenants for property on a new estate in such a way as to ensure a viable social mix on the estate' (draft revised *Code*, para. 5.6).

The mechanics of community lettings schemes generally involve special authorisation for the by-passing of certain top priority cases on the housing register in favour of 'lower need' applicants with particular desired characteristics. For example, it might be that a given proportion of larger vacancies could be set aside initially to be offered preferentially to existing estate residents needing more space, or an allocator might look down the list for the first suitable applicant in employment.

The issues raised by policies involving excluding certain applicants on grounds of potential anti-social behaviour are discussed in relation to discretionary powers in Chapter 2.

Summary

In general, social housing allocations are prioritised according to applicants' assessed housing needs. However, there are specific instances where priority is determined on other grounds. These include the promotion of lettings involving unpopular housing and those intended to contribute towards improved neighbourhood social mix.

Allocations systems can be classified in various ways. In reality, however, many systems contain elements of two or more 'ideal types'. In some cases, different prioritisation schemes are used for different groups of applicants (e.g. transfer cases and new applicants).

There are eight recognisable categories (see pp. 65–66 above) of need encompassed within most allocations systems. Whilst they are required to pay regard to specified 'reasonable preference' categories (see Chaps 5 and 6), in practice landlords retain substantial discretion in determining the measurement and weighting of these factors.

In the main, social housing allocations are determined by the application of formal rules and procedures. There are, however, various elements within most systems where there is scope for limited customer input (e.g. with respect to locational choice and willingness to be nominated to another landlord).

Matching applicants to properties is generally a two-stage process involving initial shortlisting and subsequent fine-tuning. Social landlords commonly limit the number of tenancy offers made to applicants and apply sanctions when these limits are reached.

Although there is statutory provision for appeals against exclusion from housing registers, the framework for appeals against tenancy offers (e.g. on grounds of unreasonableness) is largely subject to a landlord's own discretion.

Local lettings initiatives, usually inspired by management difficulties resulting from low demand, generally involve departing from needs-based prioritisation of applicants. Regulatory guidance places limits on the extent to which policies of this sort should be implemented.

Further reading

Allen, C., Clapham, D., Franklin, B. and Parker, J. (1997). *The Right Home? Assessing Housing Needs in Community Care*. Cardiff: Centre for Housing Management and Development, University of Cardiff.

Britain, A. and Yanetta, A. (1997). *Housing Allocations in Scotland: A Practice Note*. Edinburgh: Chartered Institute of Housing in Scotland.

Cowan, D., Pantazis, C., Gilroy, R. and Bevan, M. (1999). *Housing Sex Offenders: An Examination of Current Practice*. Coventry: Chartered Institute of Housing.

Department of the Environment, Transport and the Regions (2000) *Code of Guidance on the Allocation of Accommodation and Homelessness*. London: Stationery Office.

Griffiths, M., Parker, J., Smith, R., Stirling, T. and Trott, T. (1996). *Community Lettings: Local Allocations Policies in Practice*. York: Joseph Rowntree Foundation.

Griffiths, M., Parker, J., Smith, R. and Stirling, T. (1997). *Local Authority Housing Allocations: Systems, Policies and Procedures*. London: DETR.

Housing Corporation (1997). *Performance Standards and Regulatory Guidance for Registered Social Landlords*. London: Housing Corporation.

Parker, J. and Stirling, T. (1995). *Seen To Be Fair: A Guide to Allocating Rented Housing*. Cardiff: Housing Management Advisory Panel for Wales.

Pawson, H., Kearns, A., Keoghan, M., Malcolm, J. and Morgan, J. (1997). *Managing Voids and Difficult to Let Property*. London: Housing Corporation.

Pawson, H., Kearns, A. and Morgan, J. (1997). *Managing Voids and Difficult to Let Property: Literature Review*. London: Housing Corporation.

5.
Allocation of Local Authority Housing

Groups qualifying for 'reasonable preference' / Part
VII of HA 1996 and its interaction with Part VI / Role
of Local Government Ombudsman

Chapter 4 discusses the various approaches employed by
social landlords in allocating tenancies, and the mechanics of
needs assessment, rehousing prioritisation and matching. This
chapter focuses on the legal framework for housing allocation
in the local authority sector with respect to new tenants. In
the main, this is laid down by HA 1996 (which, as noted in
Chapter 3, has little bearing on allocations to existing tenants).

The chapter begins by outlining the categories of applicants to whom authorities are required to accord 'reasonable
preference' and goes on to discuss the interaction between
Parts VI and VII of the Act, covering housing allocations and
homelessness. It defines the legal meaning of the terms
'tenancy offer' and 'allocation' and looks at law and practice
on offers and appeals against these. Finally, it discusses the
circumstances in which the Ombudsman can become involved
in allocations decisions.

Generally speaking, local authorities are free to determine how an allocation scheme should operate. As noted in
paragraph 6.8 of the draft revised *Code of Guidance*: 'Elected
members remain responsible for determining allocations
policies and monitoring their implementation.' However, day-

to-day running of an allocations scheme and the allocation of individual properties is delegated to officers. The involvement of council members at this level is regulated under statutory instruments (see Chap. 4 and pp. 85–86 below).

Groups qualifying for 'reasonable preference'

Chapter 2 sets out the method by which local authorities select tenants to be included in their housing registers. Once that selection has been made under HA 1996 (s. 167(2)), local authority allocations systems must accord reasonable preference to the following:

1. those in insanitary or overcrowded housing;
2. those in unsatisfactory housing conditions;
3. those in conditions of temporary or insecure tenure;
4. families with dependent children or who are expecting a child;
5. households containing someone with an identified need for settled accommodation on medical or welfare grounds; and
6. households with limited opportunities to secure settled accommodation.

The *Code of Guidance* suggests that the last category 'reflects the particular difficulties that some households on a low income may have in obtaining settled accommodation for themselves in the private rented sector', settled accommodation being a long-term home rather than transient or short-term accommodation.

Since the Act came into force, the unintentionally homeless have been added as a further category to whom a reasonable preference must be given (Allocation of Housing (Reasonable and Additional Preference) Regulations 1997 (S.I. No. 1902). Furthermore, additional preference must be given to those with an identified need of housing on medical or welfare grounds who cannot reasonably be expected to find settled accommodation for themselves in the foreseeable future.

There is no precise definition of the term 'reasonable preference'. However, the draft revised *Code of Guidance* explains at paragraph 5.13 that, in this context:

> 'it means that authorities should give due weight to the factors listed in s.167(2) [see above] but it does not restrict authorities to considering only such factors. A scheme should be flexible enough to allow authorities to add other factors of their own ... However, authorities should not allow their own secondary criteria to dominate their allocations scheme at the expense of the statutory priority categories.'

There is some guidance in case-law on the meaning of the term. To give a reasonable preference means that the various criteria must be an 'important factor in making a decision about the allocation of housing' (per Tucker J in *R v Lambeth LBC, ex p Ashley* (1996)), and that 'positive favour should be shown to applications which satisfy any of the relevant criteria' (per Judge LJ in *R v Wolverhampton MBC, ex p Watters* (1997)).

A reasonable preference implies the power to choose between different applicants on 'reasonable grounds ... it is not unreasonable to prefer good tenants to bad tenants' (*R v Newham LBC, ex p Miah* (1995)). Further guidance is also contained in paragraph 5.17 of the draft revised *Code*:

> 'Authorities are required to manage the resources at their disposal prudently. They may wish to take into account the characteristics and behaviour of the people they select as tenants, both individually and collectively ... This might ... extend to selecting tenants for property on a new estate in a way that ensures a viable social mix on the estate.'

(See also Chap. 4.) Paragraph 5.12 states

> Each authority should have arrangements for determining priority in allocation between two households with similar levels of need. It would be legitimate to

employ some indicator that reflects the time spent
waiting at a particular level of need. Whatever indicators are used, they should be set out clearly in the
allocation scheme.

In *R v Islington LBC, ex p Reilly and Mannix* (1998), it was found
that any system devised must be able to take into account
multiple need factors. Paragraph 5.19 of the draft revised *Code*
states that:

'Authorities should not operate on a purely formulaic
basis. They must take into account all considerations
relevant to the housing and social needs of individual
applicants, and ignore irrelevant factors. It is open to
an authority to establish, as part of their allocations
scheme, a procedure for dealing with special cases on
an exceptional basis.'

As well as a reasonable preference, an 'additional preference' must also be afforded to those with an identified need
on medical or welfare grounds, who cannot reasonably be
expected to find settled accommodation for themselves in the
foreseeable future. Paragraph 5.14 of the draft revised *Code*
suggests that in order to secure that 'additional preference' is
given:

'an allocation scheme should ensure that such a household is accorded greater priority than householders
falling within the other priority categories. This provision does not require authorities to allocate the first
available property of any sort in such cases, but it does
assume that people meeting this description will have
first call on suitable vacancies.'

Challenge

There is no statutory right of appeal against the priority
afforded to an application by a local authority. Therefore,
challenge can only be mounted through judicial review
proceedings. Such proceedings place a heavy burden on an

applicant to demonstrate that an authority had acted unlawfully, irrationally or with *Wednesbury* unreasonableness.

Given the open textured nature of the phrase 'reasonable preference', it cannot be described as giving rise to a positive, enforceable entitlement on the part of any individual. However, it is clear that authorities cannot adopt their polices so rigidly as to fetter their discretion in considering the individual circumstances of particular applicants for housing (see e.g. *R v Canterbury City Council, ex p Gillespie* (1987); *R v Bristol City Council, ex p Johns* (1992); *R v Newham LBC, ex p Campbell* (1993); *R v Newham LBC, ex p Watkins* (1993); *R v Newham LBC, ex p Dawson* (1994); *R v Southwark LBC, ex p Melak* (1996); *R v Gateshead MBC, ex p Lauder* (1996); and *R v Lambeth LBC, ex p Ashley* (1996)).

There is no reason why an authority's own principles of allocation should not include reference to rent arrears (*R v Lambeth LBC, ex p Njomo* (1996); *R v Islington LBC, ex p Aldabbagh* (1994)). This is because arrears are a relevant consideration. Promoting those who do not otherwise qualify for a reasonable preference for irrelevant reasons is also unlawful. This has generally occurred where authorities have, for extraneous reasons, departed from their published policies.

Case report

Mrs Kingdom, a councillor for Port Talbort BC, was offered a three-bedroomed house from the council's waiting list, following her divorce which had led to her moving out of the ward she represented. Under the council's policies, as a single person she would normally have been allocated a one-bedroomed flat. The views of officers that the allocation should not be made were overridden by the chairman of the housing committee, on the basis that in order to carry out her duties as a councillor a house rather than a flat should be offered, that as there was no prospect of a two-bedroomed house, a three-bedroomed one should be offered, and that Mrs Kingdom needed to return to the ward that she represented in sufficient time to establish her presence for the next election.

> Following public concern the council sought judicial review of its own allocation. The court quashed it, declaring the tenancy void, since the allocation had been made on the basis of irrelevant considerations, while ignoring the relevant one of the needs of others who were on the waiting list. *R v Port Talbot BC, ex p Jones* (1987)

Part VII of HA 1996 and its interaction with Part VI

Parts VI and VII govern the allocation of local authority housing and local authority responsibilities for housing homeless people. Part VII of HA 1996 replaced Part III of HA 1985 (which incorporated the Housing (Homeless Persons) Act 1977). Under the new legislation, the previous obligation on local authorities to provide assistance to homeless households is retained and, in some respects, strengthened. Given the central purpose of this guide it is not appropriate to include a detailed examination of Part VII. Matters such as eligibility for assistance and the homelessness assessment process are not covered here. However, because it includes rehousing duties involving homeless households, and because of the interaction between the two parts of the Act, aspects of Part VII need to be referred to in brief.

Many of the concepts included in earlier legislation are retained in Part VII. These include matters such as 'homelessness', 'priority need' and 'intentional homelessness'. The key difference is that, under the new regime, local authorities are now under no automatic obligation to secure (long-term) housing for applicants found to be unintentionally homeless and in priority need. Instead, if the applicant is actually homeless (rather than threatened with homelessness) the authority has a *duty* to secure *temporary accommodation* for a period of two years (s. 193(2)). This duty applies where the authority is satisfied that there is no other suitable accommodation available for the applicant in the district (s. 197).

Once installed in temporary housing, the applicant's priority for permanent rehousing (allocation of a local authority tenancy or a nomination to a housing association) is assessed under Part VI alongside that of other applicants (see Chap. 2). As noted above, there is a specific requirement that local authorities, in their allocations policies, accord 'reasonable preference' to unintentionally homeless households. In practice this means that, for example, in an authority with a points-based allocations scheme, points would normally be accorded solely on the grounds of the household's status under Part VII. This would be irrespective of the household's position as regards the other reasonable preference criteria (see p. 82 above). If, at any stage during the two-year period, an applicant refuses an offer of suitable accommodation, the authority's obligations cease.

It is, of course, possible that an applicant accommodated for a limited period under section 193(2) will not be permanently rehoused within the two-year period. This might arise where the applicant has highly specific property type requirements, or because the authority's allocations scheme accords relatively little priority to the household (perhaps in view of the condition of the accommodation occupied). At this stage, the authority is under no further duty unless a fresh application is successful and a new duty occurs. Otherwise, any further period is at the authority's discretion, subject to a review of the applicant's circumstances. This review must assess whether:

1. the person continues to have a priority need;
2. there is any other suitable accommodation available in the district;
3. the applicant still requires assistance; or
4. the applicant remains eligible for assistance.

In many cases, accommodation allocated to applicants under the interim two-year duty will be local authority housing. Alternatively, it might be property managed by an RSL.

In this instance, there is a stipulation that the tenancy may not be an assured tenancy (other than an assured shorthold tenancy). Under section 209, RSLs are also prohibited from converting assured shorthold tenancies into assured tenancies in cases of this sort, except where the property is allocated to the tenant under Part VI of the Act (i.e. through the housing register). This is to ensure that the allocation of permanent tenancies, in all cases (including those involving nominations), involves consideration of the needs of homeless households alongside those of other applicants.

Other than the two-year rehousing obligation, there is also a number of other rehousing duties applying to particular categories of applicant as classified under Part VII and in particular circumstances. In some cases, these may involve the allocation of local authority housing. First, if, pending completion of enquiries, an authority has reason to believe that an applicant is:

- eligible for assistance,
- homeless, and
- in priority need,

there is an obligation to secure that suitable accommodation is available until enquiries are completed (s. 188). Secondly, where it is determined, following enquiries, that an applicant is:

- eligible for assistance,
- intentionally homeless, and
- in priority need,

authorities are required to secure that accommodation is available for a period sufficient to enable the applicant to make his or her own arrangements. In practice, this is often interpreted as a limit of 28 days.

Role of Local Government Ombudsman

If a housing applicant feels that he or she has suffered because a council has been at fault in dealing with his or her housing application, he or she may make a complaint to the Local Government Ombudsman. The Ombudsman considers whether the council has dealt with the application properly in accordance with its own policies and procedures. However, the Ombudsman does not question the merits of agreed council policies (e.g. on bedroom entitlement). The Ombudsman also normally expects the person affected to have made a complaint at a senior level within the council and given it a reasonable opportunity to reply. Many councils have their own procedures for appealing against offers of accommodation which the Ombudsman would normally expect the applicant to use.

The sorts of complaints which the Ombudsman may consider include:

- Loss of application forms and supporting documents (e.g. medical evidence)
- Delays in carrying out medical assessments
- Failure to take account of medical recommendations when making offers
- Failure to calculate housing points correctly
- Failure to calculate bedroom size entitlement properly
- Delays in making offers to high priority applicants
- Unreasonable offers of accommodation (e.g. because they do not comply with area preferences, size policy etc.)
- Failure to inform applicants of a right to appeal against unreasonable offers
- Delays in hearing appeals against unreasonable offers
- Delays in paying or failure to pay decorations allowances.

If the Ombudsman decides that a council has been administratively at fault and the applicant has suffered, he or she may recommend what the council should do to put matters right. The remedy might involve an apology and a prompt of suitable accommodation or financial compensation for time spent living in unsatisfactory accommodation and/or for time and trouble pursuing the complaint.

Two decisions provide examples of findings by the Ombudsman of maladministration. In *Complaint 97/C/2883* (LAG, August 1998, p. 21) the complainant had applied to join the housing register. The council asked the police to provide details of previous convictions of all new single applicants for housing, but without warning applicants and without obtaining their prior consent. When provided with details of the complainant's convictions, the authority excluded him from the register. The Ombudsman found the process to be unfair. First, it was outside the terms of the arrangements actually agreed with the policy, and secondly the complainant had suffered injustice because in the absence of prior warning he was deprived of the opportunity not to pursue his application.

In *Complaint 97/C/3827* (LAG, August 1998, p. 21), the local authority housing committee refused registration to the complainants. They applied for a review pursuant to section 164 of HA 1996 (see p. 30 above). The review was carried out by the same subcommittee and rejected. The reports prepared by officers for both the original and the review decisions were factually flawed and misleading. Copies of the reports had not been provided to the complainants and they had not been given the opportunity to refute them. The Ombudsman found the procedure to be unfair. The policy of the same committee considering the review as well as making the original decision did 'not accord with natural justice or good practice'.

Summary

In the construction of their allocations schemes relating to new applicants, local authorities are required to accord reasonable preference to seven specified groups. Regulatory advice and case-law provide limited guidance on the interpretation of the term 'reasonable preference'. Nevertheless, because of the generality of the concept, it does not give rise to an enforceable entitlement on the part of any individual.

As well as paying heed to the seven reasonable preference criteria, local authorities must accord additional preference on medical and/or welfare grounds.

Since there is no statutory right of appeal against housing register prioritisation, challenges to such decisions can be mounted only through judicial review.

Parts VI and VII of HA 1996 interact in important ways. Significantly, any applicant found to be unintentionally homeless and in priority need under Part VII must be given reasonable preference under Part VI. Irrespective of this, however, local authorities have specific (though limited) rehousing obligations under Part VII itself.

The Local Government Ombudsman's powers to investigate complaints of maladministration often involve cases relating to housing allocations. Examples could include, for instance, complaints over alleged failures with respect to needs identification, points calculation or information provision. Cases upheld may involve the council being recommended to provide suitable accommodation and/or pay financial compensation to the complainant.

Further reading

Arden, A. and Hunter, C. (1997). *Homelessness and Allocations: A Guide to the Housing Act 1996, Parts VI and VII* (5th edn). London: LAG.

Department of the Environment, Transport and the Regions (2000). *Code of Guidance on the Allocation of Accommodation and Homelessness*. London: Stationery Office.

Niner, P. (1997). *The Early Impact of the Housing Act 1996 and Housing Benefit Changes*. London: Shelter.

6.

Allocation of Housing by Registered Social Landlords

Reasonable preference categories and RSLs /
Nominations and assistance to local authorities /
Independence

Chapter 5 discusses the allocation of local authority housing in the context of the provisions included in Part VI of HA 1996 and the interaction with provisions on homelessness in Part VII of the same legislation.

Nominations to RSLs are of increasing significance to local authorities in complying with this legislation, particularly as the number of authorities transferring all or part of their housing stock to the RSL sector has increased. However, around half of new lettings by RSLs are not covered by nominations agreements and it is possible—indeed required by the Housing Corporation—that RSLs have independent lettings policies and practices that are consistent with their governing instruments.

This chapter clarifies the implications of the operation of these dual principles governing RSL lettings with reference to the detailed guidance provided in *Performance Standards and Regulatory Guidance for Registered Social Landlords* (3rd ed., Housing Corporation, 1997).

Reasonable preference categories and RSLs

Chapter 5 outlines the reasonable preference categories which must be applied by local authorities in determining priorities within their allocation schemes. These priorities apply to all lettings 'within the authorities' gift', including nominations to RSLs. To this extent there are close similarities in the principles to be applied to local authority lettings and to those RSL lettings covered by nominations agreements.

Performance Standards requires RSLs' lettings policies and practices for long-term rented housing to give reasonable preference to those in greatest need (Standard F2.1), again defining greatest need in relation to the seven reasonable preference categories (S.I. 1997 No. 1902; see Chap. 5). Like local authorities, RSLs may define secondary categories to be incorporated into the allocation scheme, but these must not be allowed to dominate at the expense of the primary categories. However, in the case of RSLs, the 'reasonable preference' requirement is qualified in the *Performance Standards* by the phrase 'except where this would lead to unsustainable tenancies or unstable communities'. Section 2 of the Annex to Standard F sets out the circumstances in which RSLs have some flexibility to allocate homes to groups other than those with the greatest needs (see pp. 68–72 above).

Generally, any policies which take advantage of the 'flexibility provisions' allowing departure from prioritisation solely on the basis of assessed need must record such allocations, and be reviewed by people not directly involved in allocations to ensure that flexibility is not having a discriminatory effect.

> **Example: allocating homes to applicants other than those with highest priority need**
>
> *Performance Standards* allows RSLs some flexibility in the application of priority categories to housing

allocations. RSLs wishing to allocate homes outside of their priority need criteria must take four steps:

1. Specify clearly the reasons for seeking to vary allocation policies in specific circumstances

Which specified circumstances apply?

- making better use of stock
- difficult-to-let properties
- preventing or reversing adverse social conditions.

Where the scheme falls into the third of these categories (commonly known as local lettings policies), RSLs need to act as follows (see also Chap. 2):

- define the area to which the policy applies
- specify clear objectives
- develop a broader area strategy
- set a timescale (not more than three years)
- consult with the relevant local authority
- agree through RSL board
- inform the Housing Corporation regional office.

2. Ensure that all allocations not made according to priority criteria are recorded

These lettings need to be easily identifiable on any systems (manual or computerised) used to record allocations. It must be possible to compare groups allocations are made to with those in the highest priority need for the properties concerned.

3. The operation of flexibility must be regularly and independently reviewed

There should be regular monitoring of all 'exceptional' allocations (as part of standard allocations monitoring reports). There should be independent arrangements for review of flexibility:

- monitor to ensure no discrimination occurs (e.g. black and minority ethnic households)
- include in internal audit investigations
- monitoring should involve people not directly involved in allocations

In addition, local lettings schemes should be reviewed:

- by people not directly involved in allocations
- against the specific objectives set

> • at regular intervals and at the end of three years (when an application must be made to the Housing Corporation for extension where this is required)
>
> **4. RSLs should demonstrate that policies and practices:**
> • make best use of stock
> • do not threaten community stability
> • do not involve unfairness or discrimination.

Different considerations apply to the letting of short-term rented housing provided by RSLs as temporary accommodation for the homeless. Priority should be given to households for whom the local authority has accepted a temporary duty to accommodate or a duty to secure accommodation under Part VII of HA 1996, and to those eligible for long-term housing but unlikely to get it in the near future (Interpretation of Standard F2.1).

Nominations and assistance to local authorities

The reasonable preference categories set the parameters for the relationship between RSLs and local authorities, since they apply to 50 per cent or more of RSL lettings. There are further requirements for RSLs to co-operate with and assist local authorities in relation to lettings policies and practices. These are detailed in Chapter 2 at pp. 39–40.

In addition, RSLs are 'encouraged to join Common Housing Registers where this is considered appropriate but not to enter into common allocation policies unless the governing body has agreed that this would not threaten the RSL's objectives and independence' (Interpretation of Standard F1.1). Similarly, while RSLs may enter into arrangements that offer more than 50 per cent nominations, 'the Corporation is concerned that nomination agreements should not remove the RSL's independence' (Interpretation of Standard F3.2).

The relationship with local authorities is of central importance in housing needs assessment, both generally and relation to particular needs such as those of black and minority ethnic (BME) groups. For example, the Housing Corporation's *BME Housing Policy* (1998) states that 'where local authorities have local BME policies, we encourage RSLs to work within these policies'.

More generally, as part of their local accountability arrangements, RSLs are expected to participate in local liaison arrangements, consult the local authority on funding bids and provide information on performance and co-operate with the local authority on regeneration and area renewal strategies (Interpretation of Standard B4). All of these obligations may have a bearing on allocation activities.

In practice, most RSLs do have close working relationships with local authority partners through, for example, social housing liaison groups, social housing compacts and joint commissioning groups. The public spending framework for social housing announced in the government's Comprehensive Spending Review in the Summer of 1998 is likely to further increase the importance of local authority partnerships for RSLs. The majority of public funding opportunities for RSLs are likely to derive from local authority initiatives rather than through the Housing Corporation.

Example: lettings policies for supported housing

Performance Standards allows RSLs to operate different lettings policies for each type of supported housing and to vary policies according to the type, level and mix of each project. This enables RSLs to be accountable, without threatening the security of potentially sensitive local operations (e.g. involving ex-offenders or substance abusers). To comply with *Performance Standards* RSLs must:

1.(a) hold a central lettings policy:
- outlining the general approach to lettings, and
- recognising responsibilities to and agreements with local authorities and other partners

(b) consult with relevant local authorities
(c) agree through RSL Board;
2. allocate vacancies in individual schemes in accordance with the general policy, and:
• reflect type, level and mix of needs catered for
• discharge responsibilities to local authorities and others
• set numerical targets for move-on departures; and
3. Monitor and review all lettings to ensure that:
• there is compliance with general policy
• the project's aims and objectives are being achieved
• local priority needs are being met
• discrimination and unfairness is avoided
• best use is made of stock and specialist support staff
• policy implementation assists in building community stability.

Independence

Throughout the guidance provided to RSLs on lettings in *Performance Standards* is an emphasis on the importance of independence. This section explores the issues associated with RSL independence in more detail in order to identify any differences in emphasis which may arise in RSLs' allocations policies and practices. It considers in turn the issues of accountability, specialisation and performance.

Accountability

RSLs are expected to have in place arrangements which demonstrate appropriate levels of accountability to those to whom they have a wider responsibility, including local authorities (Standard B4), and must consult authorities on changes to letting policies (Standard F1.1).

However, *Performance Standards* stresses a primary accountability to RSLs' governing instruments in order to preserve their independence. Thus Standard F1.1 requires written

lettings policies which must be consistent with the association's governing instruments. Similarly, reservations on
participation in common allocation systems (Standard F1.1)
or in granting high levels of nominations to local authorities
(Standard F3.2) are expressed in terms of the need to protect
RSLs' aims and objectives and independence. The governing
bodies of RSLs are charged with responsibility for ensuring
that any allocations arrangements entered into are consistent
with governing instruments and do not compromise their
independence.

Specialisation

Associated with the prime accountability to each RSL's
governing instrument is recognition that the 2,000 or so RSLs
are very different from one another. They can have differing
patterns of specialisation, partly as a result of the roots of some
associations in voluntary action to meet very specific types of
need or to serve particular geographical areas.

Some of these differences are reflected in compliance
arrangements for *Performance Standards*. For example, the duty
to co-operate with local authorities on homelessness is qualified by the phrase 'within reason' (Standard F3.1). The interpretation clarifies that what is reasonable depends on the RSL's
housing stock, resources and skills and on agreement on
financial arrangements. Thus, where homelessness need is
predominantly for family accommodation, some RSLs specialising in sheltered housing might claim exemption on the
ground that they are not geared up to assist homeless people.
Similarly, very small RSLs (which qualify for a more limited
form of regulation under the Regulatory Arrangements for
Small Associations (RASA) regime) are spared the duty to
consult local authorities on their letting policies (Standard
F1.1).

In contrast it would be quite unreasonable for stock
transfer RSLs, which account for a significant proportion of
social lettings in their areas of operation, to be exempt from

any of the duties to co-operate with, assist and consult the local housing authority. Varying models of division of responsibilities between the local authority and the RSL for managing housing registers, and administering homelessness services such as temporary accommodation, have emerged in stock transfer areas. However, close co-operation is essential to meet duties under HA 1996 and *Performance Standards*.

More significant differences are reflected in the separate performance standards set for supported housing. While these follow the same format as for general needs housing, there are differences in the detail. For example:

1. Supported housing which is not intended to be a permanent home should have move-on policies and numerical targets for departures (Standard F2.2).
2. While RSLs may have different lettings policies for each type of supported housing, they can choose to publish a central policy outlining the general approach to letting supported housing, thereby avoiding publication of potentially sensitive policies for specific schemes (Standard F1.1).
3. Supported housing projects are also expected to set numerical targets for the number of departures each year, to ensure that specialist support resources are used effectively and that residents have the opportunity to move on to general needs housing (Standard F2.2).

Further issues arise where RSLs have been set up to meet the needs of very specific groups of 'beneficiaries' which may be stated in their governing instruments, charitable objectives (for Charity Commission registration) or articles of association.

Great care is required in balancing these objectives against Housing Corporation requirements that 'RSLs should let their homes in ways that are fair and non-discriminatory' (Standard F1.3).

In general, housing cannot be provided for particular racial groups exclusively, unless a 'special need' can be identified. Chapter 7 discusses the circumstances in which it is legal for positive action to be taken to secure housing provision to particular racial groups. In practice, the Housing Corporation's *BME Housing Policy* defines BME associations as those which draw at least 80 per cent of their governing body from BME communities. Analyses of lettings by BME associations between 1989/90 and 1996/97 indicate that between 45 and 88 per cent of lettings are made to BME households. Thus, neither governing body membership nor letting activity are normally confined to particular racial groups.

Performance

The final aspect of RSLs' independence in allocations relates to their responsibility for performance in implementing their letting policies. The principle of organisational responsibility applies even where the administration of certain functions, such as housing register administration, has effectively been delegated to another body.

RSLs must ensure that their processes for selection and allocation are effectively controlled and accurately recorded (Standard F1.2). This means that there must be clear arrangements for delegation of responsibilities, both within the RSL and (where necessary) with other agencies.

In relation to internal delegation, the administration of allocation procedures in RSLs is often the subject of independent review through the internal audit process. Techniques such as audit trails and bypass monitoring may be used to establish that policies and procedures are followed in practice.

In relation to external delegations, some CHRs operate with contracts or service level agreements between partners and the organisation running the register, so that RSLs can be absolutely clear on the basis of delegation.

Recording information about lettings is partly facilitated through participation of RSLs in the Continuous Recording (CORE) system which is a requirement for RSLs with 250 or more homes in management. This can enable RSLs to demonstrate that lettings are in line with their policies. However, more sophisticated data is required to enable the overall allocations process, from applications to offers and lettings, to be monitored and reviewed. This is discussed further in Chapter 8.

A particular emphasis of *Performance Standards* is the need for allocation procedures to be fair and non-discriminatory. RSLs must avoid restrictions on access to housing which are irrelevant to housing and support needs (Standard F1.3) and meet obligations under the Sex Discrimination Act 1975, the Race Relations Act 1976 and the Disability Discrimination Act 1995 (see Chap. 7 for discussion of this legislation).

> **Example: instances in which RSLs may exclude applicants from rehousing**
>
> Annex 3 of the Housing Corporation's *Performance Standards* interprets Standard F1.3 and identifies certain limited circumstances in which RSLs may exclude applicants from consideration. These include:
> * evidence of tenancy breaches in previous two years
> * violence against staff or residents in previous two years
> * the applicant is unable to meet conditions of occupancy (and support to do so is not available)
> * the applicant is not in need of special adaptations or support services provided with the property.

As a compliance test on non-discrimination, the Housing Corporation monitors the percentage of lettings to BME households and compares this to Census data in the landlords' area of operation. It makes enquiries of RSLs with outlying areas of performance.

Independent Housing Ombudsman

The Independent Housing Ombudsman was established by HA 1996, replacing the Housing Association Tenants Ombudsman Service, and operates as an independent company funded by subscriptions from RSLs. Housing Corporation Circular

R5-03/97 requires all RSLs to be in membership, and by March 1998, 2,148 landlords managing 1.2 million properties had registered their membership. There is also a small number of private sector landlords in voluntary membership of the scheme.

Like the Local Government Ombudsman (see Chap. 5), the Independent Housing Ombudsman responds to enquiries from tenants, some of which (about 20 per cent in 1997/98) are investigated as formal complaints. However, there is a greater emphasis on resolving complaints through informal settlement, mediation and arbitration, and only a small minority of cases (5 per cent of all complaints subject to formal scrutiny in 1997/98) involve an Ombudsman's Final Determination on maladministration or a formal enquiry report.

Nearly one fifth of all complaints scrutinised by the Independent Housing Ombudsman involve transfers or allocations, and there are further cases of relevance involving nuisance or harassment. The Ombudsman comments on the number of complaints involving transfers and that 'although there is good practice guidance on allocations and on administering waiting lists of applicants, surprisingly little has been written about administering transfers'. Examples of transfer and allocations complaints include excessive waiting times for transfers from overcrowded accommodation, and communication errors in nominations procedures.

Summary

As in the local authority sector, lettings by RSLs are subject to requirements that they are made in line with the 'reasonable preference' criteria specified in HA 1996 (as subsequently amended by statutory instrument). In specific circumstances, however, RSLs have discretion to depart from these principles.

Under a variety of legal and regulatory obligations, RSLs are required to co-operate closely with local authorities with respect to allocations. Nevertheless, RSLs are also expected to retain a degree of independence and to reserve their primary accountability to their governing instruments. This restricts the degree to which RSLs should, for example, subjugate their own allocations priorities as participants in CHRs.

RSLs are subject to specific regulatory requirements to implement allocations procedures in fair and non-discriminatory ways. Reflecting the *Code of Guidance* for local authorities, however, the Housing Corporation allows RSLs discretion to exclude a limited range of groups from access to housing.

The Independent Housing Ombudsman, set up in 1997, has jurisdiction over RSLs and their allocations and management practices. Initial experience suggests that a significant element of the Ombudsman's case-load will involve complaints relating to housing allocations.

Further reading

Commission for Racial Equality (1989). *Positive Action and Racial Equality in Housing*. London, CRE.

Housing Corporation (1997). *Performance Standards and Regulatory Guidance for Registered Social Landlords, Third Edition Incorporating Statutory Management Guidance Under s36 of Housing Act 1996*. London: Housing Corporation.

Housing Corporation (1998). *Black and Minority Ethnic Housing Policy*. London: Housing Corporation.

Independent Housing Ombudsman (1998). *Annual Report and Accounts 97–98*. London: Independent Housing Ombudsman Ltd.

Mullins, D. and Niner, P. (1996). *Common Housing Registers: An Evaluation and Analysis of Current Practice*. London: Housing Corporation.

7.
Discrimination in Allocations

Introduction—rationing and discrimination /
Unlawful discrimination / Applying equal
opportunities in allocations

Introduction—rationing and discrimination

This chapter examines the role of discrimination in the
allocations process and defines the distinction between lawful
and unlawful practices in this regard. It looks at the ways that
social landlords can counter the danger of illegal discrimination, including the role of equal opportunities policies,
record-keeping and monitoring. In common with the book as
a whole, the chapter is intended to address housing managers'
practical concerns and responsibilities. Unlike some of the
other chapters, however, it may be that some aspects of it will
also be of interest to policy-makers.

As discussed Chapter 1, in most areas and for most of
the post-war period, social housing has been in scarce supply,
and approaches to allocations have essentially been concerned
with rationing. As the Cullingworth Committee commented
in 1969, in this context the whole basis of allocations was
discriminatory: certain applicants were selected, while others
were refused. During certain periods the need for rationing
led to the development of explicitly discriminatory practices,

and identifiable groups of housing applicants were treated differently from others. More often there were discriminatory outcomes from policies and procedures which were not necessarily formulated with a discriminatory intent.

Perhaps of equal importance, the issue of scarcity is the differentiated nature of housing supply. While the residualisation process, referred to in Chapter 1, has significantly reduced the stock of the most desirable properties (e.g. houses with gardens), recent years have seen increasing recognition that a significant proportion of the social housing stock in certain areas is becoming difficult to let. New approaches, such as community lettings and marketing, are being applied to such properties at the same time as a needs-based rationing approach is applied to the remainder of the stock. This raises possibilities of new forms of discrimination. Similar risks attach to policies—mainly inspired by pressure from central government—to incentivise moves by tenants considered to be 'underoccupiers' (see Chap. 3).

There is an enormous research literature documenting the ways in which scarcity and heterogeneity have been managed to produce discriminatory results. The elimination of discrimination has been recognised as a necessary element of housing allocations policies for at least 30 years (e.g. 1969 Cullingworth Report). Evidence of continued discrimination against ethnic minorities, single parent households and other identifiable groups has been found in many research studies. The current context for housing allocations outlined in this chapter includes elements which, left unchecked, will make for further discrimination.

Needs-based allocation systems have contributed to the development of a residualised social housing sector, increasingly catering for socially excluded groups among whom some ethnic minorities and single parent households are disproportionately represented. Only policies to improve the overall quality and status of social housing can eliminate the housing discrimination faced by these groups, who depend on it for access to decent homes. But over and above this, specific measures are required to ensure that ethnic minorities and other disadvantaged groups have fair access to the full range of social housing, rather than being concentrated in its worst sectors.

Measures to eliminate discrimination are supported by legislation (e.g. the Race Relations and Sex Discrimination Acts), Codes of Practice (e.g. *Race Relations Code of Practice in Rented Housing*), regulations (e.g. the Housing Corporation *Performance Standards*) and other good practice guidance (e.g. *CIH Housing Management Standards Manual*). This guide draws on these sources and identifies good practice to ensure that the dangers outlined above are recognised and responded to.

Unlawful discrimination

Three main areas of discrimination are restricted by legislation: race discrimination; sex discrimination; and discrimination against those with disabilities. This legislation applies to allocation by all social landlords. The control of discrimination is dealt in a similar way within the structure of the legislation governing these three areas, and specific provision is made within the Acts to deal with unlawful discrimination in housing allocation.

The Commission for Racial Equality (CRE) has issued a *Code of Practice in Rented Housing* (1991) defining and giving examples of the various categories of racial discrimination, and identifying the good practice steps which landlords should take to prevent discrimination arising. So far as allocations by local housing authorities are concerned, Chapter 22 of the DETR's draft revised *Code of Guidance* draws attention to the Sex Discrimination Act 1975 (SDA), the Race Relations Act 1976 (RRA) and the Disability Discrimination Act 1995 (DDA) and outlines the main provisions contained in them. A more detailed account of discrimination may be found in A. Kilpatrick, *Discrimination in Social Housing* (2000).

Discrimination in allocations

Each of the three Acts contains specific provisions which render discrimination in allocation unlawful (SDA, s. 30; RRA, s. 21; DDA, s. 22). Each section provides that it is unlawful for a person (which includes companies and local authorities as well as individuals) to discriminate against another in the disposal of property:

1. in the terms on which those premises are offered; or
2. by refusing the application for those premises; or
3. in the treatment of an applicant in relation to any list of persons in need of premises of that description.

For these purposes 'disposal' means the grant of any right of occupation, whether by way of ownership or otherwise, and whether granting a tenancy or licence.

Also relevant in allocation is the fact that it is unlawful for a person who manages premises to discriminate in the way he or she affords access to any benefits or facilities relating to the premises, or by refusing or deliberately omitting to afford access to them.

Racial and sexual discrimination

Racial and sexual discrimination may be *direct* or *indirect*.

Direct discrimination

This is caused, in the case of sex discrimination, by treating a person less favourably than someone of the opposite sex would be treated (SDA, ss. 1(1)(a), 2(1)). In the case of racial discrimination it is caused by treating a person less favourably on racial grounds than any other person would be treated (RRA, s. 1(1)(a)). 'Racial grounds' means race, colour, nationality or ethnic or national origins (RRA, s. 3(1)). Segregation on racial grounds is treated as direct discrimination (RRA, s. 1(1)(a)).

Examples given in the CRE's *Code of Practice for Rented Housing* include where a housing association allocates a poorer standard property to a black applicant than to a white applicant on racial grounds, and where a local authority rehouses one group of homeless persons staying in temporary accommodation at a slower rate than others because of their ethnic or racial origin.

The term 'ethnic' is to be construed in a broad cultural and historic sense. Thus Sikhs are a group defined by reference to ethnic origins (*Mandla v Dowell Lee* (1983)), as are gypsies (*CRE v Dutton* (1989)). However, rastafarians are not an ethnic group (*Crown Suppliers PSA v Dawkins* (1991)). As a racial group can be defined by colour, it may be of more than one ethnic origin (*Lambeth LBC v CRE* (1990)).

Indirect discrimination

This occurs where a requirement or condition is applied which, although applied equally to persons of all racial groups or of both sexes, is such that:

1. a considerably smaller proportion of a particular sex or racial group can comply with it than others, and
2. it cannot be shown to be justifiable irrespective of the colour, race, nationality or ethnic or national origins or sex of the person to whom it is applied, and
3. it is to the detriment of that other because he or she cannot comply with it.

Indirect discrimination is unlawful whether or not the effect of the requirement or condition is appreciated and whether or not the effect is intended. An example of indirect discrimination given in the CRE's *Code of Practice for Rented Housing* is where a landlord requires a lengthy period of local residence before an applicant can be considered for rehousing. In an appropriate case such a rule may disproportionately affect members of ethnic minorities who may have settled in the area recently. A formal CRE investigation of homelessness and discrimination in Tower Hamlets found that the treatment of separated families where some members were resident outside the UK was found to represent indirect discrimination against

Bangladeshi applicants. This, in combination with other evidence of direct discrimination, led to a non-discrimination notice being served on the council.

Disability discrimination

Only direct discrimination is relevant to the disabled. 'Disability' means a physical or mental impairment which has a substantial and long-term adverse effect on a person's ability to carry out normal day-to-day activities (DDA, s. 1). Discrimination occurs where a person treats a disabled person less favourably for a reason which relates to his or her disability than someone without that disability would be treated (s. 24(1)(a)). If the treatment can be justified there is no discrimination (s. 24(1)(b)). Treatment is justified if the person letting the property is satisfied that the necessary conditions arise and it is reasonable for him or her to hold that position (s. 24(2)). The necessary conditions are set out in section 24(3) and are as follows:

1. the treatment is necessary so as not to endanger the health or safety of any (including the disabled) person;
2. the disabled person is incapable of entering into an enforceable agreement, or of giving informed consent, and accordingly the treatment is reasonable;
3. where limiting access to any benefits or facilities, the treatment is necessary in order for the disabled person or occupiers of other premises within the building to make use of the benefit or facility; and/or
4. where refusing or deliberately omitting to afford access to benefits or facilities, the treatment is necessary in order for other occupiers of premises within the building to make use of them.

Victimisation

It is unlawful to discriminate by victimising a person (SDA, s. 2; RRA, s. 4; DDA, s. 55). Victimisation occurs if a person is given less favourable treatment than others in the same circumstances because it is suspected or known that he or she has brought proceedings under one of the Acts, or given evidence or information relating to such proceedings or alleged that discrimination has occurred.

Special cases

Consent to assignment and subletting

It is unlawful to discriminate when considering the question of whether to consent to subletting or assignment of a right of occupation (RRA, s. 24; SDA, s. 31). It is also unlawful to discriminate in the terms upon which consent is given.

Other methods of unlawful discrimination

Unlawful discrimination in the grant of rights of occupation may occur by contravention of more general provisions prohibiting discrimination in connection with the provision of goods, facilities or services to the public, either by refusing a person access to such goods etc., or by offering access on other than the same terms as access to them is offered to others (SDA, s. 29; RRA, s. 20; DDA, s. 19). Included in the phrase 'facilities and services' is accommodation in a hotel, boarding house or other similar establishment.

Sex discrimination by voluntary and other bodies

There is a general exemption for voluntary bodies and charities which are set up to provide, or have among their objects the provision of, benefits for one sex only (SDA, s. 34). Further exemptions are provided for hospitals and reception centres for people requiring special care, supervision or attention; for premises used for the purposes of an organised religion, where separation of the sexes is a part of the religion; or where facilities provided are such that sexual embarrassment or objection might result. Finally, there is an exemption for premises where the accommodation provided is 'communal' accommodation, provided that men and women are treated fairly and equitably given the circumstances.

Applying equal opportunities in allocations

This section considers action to secure equal opportunities and eliminate unlawful discrimination in allocations at a number of levels. It begins at the national level by considering legal remedies, including the issue of non-discrimination notices by the CRE, and continues by considering the (limited) scope for positive action to redress past discrimination. It then proceeds to discuss local level initiatives including explicit policy commitment, consultation, needs assessment, staff training, policy review and monitoring.

Legal remedies for unlawful discrimination

Action in the county court

Where unlawful discrimination has occurred the victim may take proceedings for breach of statutory duty in the county court (SDA, s. 66; RRA, s. 57; DDA, s. 25) and seek a declaration that an act is unlawful and/or an injunction and/or damages.

Non-discrimination notices

Where a complaint of sex discrimination is made out the Equal Opportunities Commission (EOC) may issue a non-discrimination notice. In the case of race discrimination, the CRE has similar powers. In both cases the notices are enforceable in the county court. There is no equivalent power for the disabled.

One of the most widely known investigations of racial discrimination in housing allocations was that undertaken by the CRE in Hackney, published in 1984. It found direct racial discrimination in the allocation system whereby white applicants, from each demand group, consistently received better quality properties than did black and minority ethnic groups. The CRE issued a non-discrimination notice with the following requirements:

- Keeping of ethnic records and their subsequent monitoring
- Setting-up of relevant training programmes
- Review of procedures and practices operated and the criteria used in assessing which applicants and tenants would be offered available property
- Assignment of a senior official in the housing department who would be responsible for ensuring the council's compliance with the non-discrimination notice and with the RRA generally.

These requirements have widespread application, and have subsequently been adopted and expanded on in most good practice guidance on eliminating discrimination in housing (e.g. *Code of Practice in Rented Housing*).

Scope for positive action in allocations

In general, housing cannot be provided for particular racial groups exclusively unless a 'special need' can be identified. Special needs cannot be defined by reference to colour. Thus charitable instruments which limit the charity's purpose by reference to colour are to be reinterpreted as if they do not (RRA, s. 34). However, it is possible for housing organisations specifically established to meet the needs of particular racial groups (defined without reference to colour) to operate under three separate RRA provisions.

First, groups operating on a membership basis (e.g. housing co-operatives) can limit membership by racial group (other than colour) if this is their main object (s. 26). Secondly, positive action schemes designed to meet special needs of particular racial groups in affording access to facilities or services to meet such needs with regard to education, training or welfare can also be developed (s. 35); however, these schemes are by definition temporary, lasting only as long as the special need can be demonstrated. Thirdly, it is possible for a housing association set up as a charitable body to confer benefits on persons of a class defined other than by reference to colour (s. 34). The section is probably wide enough to cover, for example, the provision of hostel accommodation.

The 1989 CRE publication *Positive Action and Racial Equality in Housing* advises use of section 34 over section 35, since periodic examination of whether a special need continues to exist is not necessary.

National and local policy frameworks

Frameworks for eliminating unlawful discrimination at the local level are provided by the *Housing Investment Programme (HIP) Guidance* (for local authorities), *Performance Standards*, and supporting policies such as the *Black and Minority Ethnic Housing Policy* (for RSLs) and more general guidance such as the *Code of Practice in Rented Housing*, the Local Government Management Board's *Equal Opportunities Checklist* and the National Housing Federation's *Promoting Diversity, Choice and Involvement* (see 'Further reading' below).

The *HIP Guidance* was strengthened in 1998 to indicate the importance attached by central government to equality of opportunity in housing provision across all sectors. It went on to encourage local authorities to develop policies covering the needs of black and minority ethnic communities in their housing strategies. This was supported by the Housing Corporation's *Black and Minority Ethnic Housing Policy* which states:

> Where local housing authorities have local BME policies, we encourage RSLs to work within these policies. Where local authorities are developing local BME policies or have not yet developed policies, we will work with them. We will also encourage RSLs to participate in the development of locally based housing strategies that will achieve the aims of our policy at a local level.

However, in the year prior to the issue of this guidance, a survey conducted on designing local housing strategies (Goss and Blackaby, 1998) found that only half of local authority housing strategies (56 per cent) dealt with equal opportunity issues in general, whilst only 37 per cent consider race and housing and 26 per cent gender and housing. Thus there is scope for authorities to set the framework for eliminating unlawful discrimination by incorporating fuller policy commitments to these issues into their housing strategies.

Consultation

As the *HIP Guidance* states: 'It is impossible to develop a good strategy without involving all those who are affected by decisions arising from development of the strategy.' Consultation should be with both service users and local 'stakeholder' interest groups. But again the survey of strategies by Goss and Blackaby demonstrated shortcomings in relation to equal opportunities. The proportion of authorities consulting service users about their housing strategy reached 60 per cent consulting users with disabilities, 39 per cent BME users, and 33 per cent women users. Meanwhile, 37 per cent consulted women's organisations and 32 per cent consulted with BME organisations (as stakeholders) in preparing their housing strategy. Thus there is scope for greater involvement of external organisations in shaping the equal opportunities elements of housing strategies.

Identifying housing needs

Consultation with service users, advice agencies and community groups can provide a useful source of information in identifying housing (including hidden) needs which is an essential element of ensuring that housing allocation systems do not discriminate. Other elements required to construct a sufficient picture of housing needs and variations between groups include:

- Use of Census data and other national survey data such as the Survey of English Housing
- Analysis of housing register data and comparison with external data
- Carrying out housing needs surveys (both general and specific to particular needs groups such as people with disabilities and BME groups)
- Collecting qualitative data through research, focus groups, user panels and consultation with community organisations
- Information collected through service monitoring systems such as ethnic record-keeping and monitoring (see below).

Staff training

Staff training was a key area highlighted by the CRE's formal investigation in Hackney, and has continued to be emphasised in subsequent good practice guidance. This reflects the important role of allocations staff in information giving, decision-making and record-keeping—all of which can have a significant impact on user experience of the allocations process. While some approaches to allocations have sought to minimise the extent and monitor the exercise of officer discretion, it has been increasingly recognised that discretion and judgement are the central resources available to allocators to balance the competing demands made of them.

If this is the case, training becomes central to the elimination of unlawful discrimination. The Local Government Management Board has produced a checklist for housing departments including guidance on induction for new employees and training and staff development issues. Detailed guidance on race equality training for housing association staff (CRE, 1993) includes the following:

- A senior staff member should be responsible for training
- The overall equal opportunities training strategy should include induction, recruitment and selection and specific topics such as racial harassment

- Customer care and quality assurance training should incorporate a race equality dimension
- The race equality element of training should include prejudice and discrimination, legislation, ethnic record-keeping and dealing with discriminatory remarks from the public
- Training should be relevant to staff's day-to-day work.

Review of policies and procedures

The Best Value principles which local authorities are now expected to apply to service provision require that authorities and other public services providers, such as RSLs, undertake regular service reviews to ensure that these meet with the needs of the public and are provided in the most efficient and effective ways. An independent audit element is integral to this approach. There is also a wealth of good practice guidance on the need for regular review of policies and procedures to ensure that unlawful discrimination is not occurring and to enable corrective action to be taken where it is. Thus continuous improvement principles should extend to equity objectives as well as effectiveness objectives (see Chap. 8).

Applying Best Value principles to ensure that services do not discriminate should involve service users and minority organisations in touch with those who may not currently use services. There is also a role for independent research studies. In the past such studies have illuminated the range of ways in which discrimination may arise, for example through:

- Procedures such as residential qualifications and home visit assessments which may have an indirectly discriminatory effect
- Competing priorities such as the need to minimise empty properties which may conflict with the goal of providing fair access to the best housing for all groups, and
- The impact of wider societal values in discretionary decision processes which may lead to certain groups such as single parents and large families receiving unfavourable treatment.

Such studies can provide a valuable addition to internal monitoring processes which should provide the basic data necessary for ongoing service review. The example of ethnic record-keeping and monitoring (ERKM) illustrates this.

Ethnic record-keeping and monitoring

ERKM is a key method of assessing who is applying for and who is receiving social housing. Its principles were succinctly stated by the Cullingworth Committee in 1969, which recommended that 'records be kept and used to establish how many coloured [*sic*] people were applying for council houses, how many were getting them, and what type and quality of house they were obtaining'.

The CRE *Code* recommends that in order to determine whether an organisation is providing housing and services on an equitable basis, it needs to maintain an ERKM system and that local authorities, housing associations and co-operatives, housing action trusts and other large landlords keep ethnic records and monitor them on a regular basis.

Where the organisation or the ethnic minority population is very small, naturally only a fairly basic system is needed to establish the number of applicants and to produce an annual report. The problem of small numbers can be addressed by using time series analysis, combining the periods (e.g. individual quarters) to give a large enough sample for meaningful analysis. Additionally, ethnic origin classifications can be collapsed into a small number of categories, such as 'Black' and 'White', to enable some simple comparisons to be made even where numbers are small.

What classification system should be used?

This raises the general problem that no ethnic classifications are entirely satisfactory since ethnicity is a social construct which may be interpreted differently by different people. Because of this applicants should always be asked to define their own ethnic group (from a list of options). Which classifications are to be used depends on the ethnic make-up of the area (e.g. local areas may have significant communities, such as Somalis or Yemenis) whose needs should be identified by a more detailed ethnic origin breakdown than is provided by the Census.

The 1991 Census represents the first time a specific ethnic origin question was asked in a Census. The categories used were:

White	Pakistani
Black Caribbean	Bangladeshi
Black African	Chinese
Black Other	Any other ethnic group
Indian	

Whilst more detailed subdivisions of the 'Black Other' and 'Other' classifications are available, these broader descriptions are often sufficient. However, if these categories are to be used to set performance targets, it may be more relevant to use CORE categories (used on RSL CORE lettings returns), providing data regarding housing allocations, which are somewhat different. CORE uses a two-stage classification:

Asian	Black
Caribbean	White
African	Other
South-East Asian	Mixed
British/European	
Irish	
Other	
Combination	
Refused	

What should be monitored?

At the most basic level, housing providers (both local authorities and RSLs) should monitor the following:

- *Homelessness*: applications; acceptances; use of temporary accommodation; permanent rehousing

- *Other applications*:   waiting list; transfer list
- *Allocations*:   offers; acceptances; refusals; HA nominations (for local authorities only)

Ideally, use of housing advice (and type of advice sought), housing benefits, repairs and improvements and quality of property allocated should also be monitored.

What about property quality?

A number of different methods can be used to generate a quality index against which lettings can be monitored (see Mullins, 1991). For example, one London borough gave scores for three factors: property amenities, block environment, and wider local environment. Detailed questionnaires were completed by estate management staff and the data analysed by the research section to produce a ranking order. Another housing authority used a simpler method based on gradings of all estates by lettings officers in terms of how easily they could be let. A third, and probably the most common, method of developing a quality index is to set up a points system for various property and environment factors.

One of the main limitations found in ERKM systems is the lack of emphasis placed on regular monitoring and review. Without such activity there is little point in collecting the information in the first place. Chapter 8 therefore provides further guidance on the ways in which ERKM systems can be used by comparing performance against targets.

Summary

The need for rationing social housing means that the allocation process is inherently one which involves discrimination in favour of some individuals or groups at the expense of others. A body of legislation exists to restrict the ability of local authorities and RSLs to abuse their power as landlords by exercising discrimination illegitimately in the housing allocations process, for example on grounds of race, sex or disability.

Unlawful discrimination can be direct or indirect. The latter may involve the imposition of rules or procedures not necessarily intended to disadvantage one group by comparison with others.

As well as recourse to legal remedies against unlawful discrimination, the practical application of equal opportunities principles in housing allocations can involve positive action in favour of groups at risk of being disadvantaged. In addition, it is important that landlords consider the needs of such groups in the process of housing strategy formulation and consult with relevant community organisations. Staff training, together with ERKM, also have important roles to play.

Further reading

Commission for Racial Equality (1984). *Race and Council Housing in Hackney*. London: CRE.

Commission for Racial Equality (1989). *Positive Action and Racial Equality in Housing*. London: CRE.

Commission for Racial Equality (1991). *Code of Practice for Rented Housing*. London: CRE.

Commission for Racial Equality (1993). *Housing Associations and Racial Equality*. London: CRE.

Commission for Racial Equality (1998). *A Formal Investigation of Homelessness and Discrimination in Tower Hamlets*. London: CRE.

Cullingworth Committee (1969). *Council Housing Purposes, Procedures and Priorities*. London: Department of Environment and Welsh Office.

Housing Corporation, The (1998). *Black and Minority Ethnic Housing Policy*. London: Housing Corporation.

Goss, S. and Blackaby, B. (1998). *Designing Local Housing Strategies*. Coventry: CIH/Local Government Association.

Jones, A. (1996). *Making Monitoring Work: a Handbook for Racial Equality Practitioners*. Coventry: Centre for Research in Ethnic Relations, University of Warwick.

Kilpatrick, A. (2000). *Discrimination in Social Housing*. London: Lemos and Crane, Arden's Housing Library.

Local Government Management Board (1991). *Equal Opportunities Checklist for Housing Departments*. Luton: Local Government Management Board.

Mullins, D. (1991). *Accounting For Equality—A Handbook on Ethnic Monitoring in Housing*. London: CRE.

National Housing Federation (1998). *Promoting Diversity, Choice and Involvement—a New Vision for a Black and Minority Ethnic Housing Policy*. London: NHF.

8.
Monitoring of Allocations

Introduction and context / Objectives of monitoring / Monitoring in practice / Performance indicators / Fraudulent applications

Introduction and context

This chapter outlines some of the ways in which social landlords can monitor the allocations process to ensure that their policy objectives are achieved in practice and, more generally, to assess activity with respect to the 'four Es' (efficiency, economy, effectiveness and equity). It also deals with the specific legal provisions concerning fraudulent applications. Although it is intended to be of practical relevance to front-line housing staff and their managers, the chapter is also directed towards the interests of policy-makers to a greater extent than other parts of the book.

Approaches to performance monitoring in social housing have become much more sophisticated in recent years as a result of improved information technology (IT), an increased policy emphasis on performance and the influence of new public management ideas on practice.

IT developments have included the emergence of integrated housing management information systems, and more accessible interrogation packages enabling system users to make greater use of administrative data for monitoring purposes.

A key stimulus to this has been the imposition of external requirements on landlords to provide information on performance. Examples include the development of Reports to Tenants under section 167 of the Local Government and Housing Act 1989. This requires local authorities to provide tenants each year with 'such information as may be determined by the Secretary of State relating to the functions of the authority as a local housing authority during the year'. Specific requirements under this determination include the numbers of properties let during the previous year to various classes of applicants, and the average relet interval for properties let during the year. A similar regime of reports for RSL tenants was introduced under the Tenants' Guarantee in 1994.

Other external influences include the development of local authority performance indicators under the Citizens Charter from 1993/94, and in the development of performance indicators for the largest RSLs by the Housing Corporation from 1994. All of these regimes include simple indicators related to allocations. For example, Housing Corporation published performance indicators include relet times, and the proportion of lettings to local authority nominees, BME households and statutory homeless households.

The spread of new public management ideas has made practitioners more conscious of the potential of performance monitoring as a tool for improving services. The split between client and contractor functions arising from the introduction of compulsory competitive tendering in housing management provided a major stimulus to the specification of services and the quantification of outputs. Ideas of continuous improvement of services have been taken up by managers, and the development of the Best Value regime by the Labour Government has provided a fillip to performance benchmarking to provide more meaningful comparisons between peer groups of organisations with similar operating contexts and characteristics.

Objectives of monitoring

In this context the objectives of monitoring allocations may be defined as:
  1. enhancing accountability to external audiences such as tenants and applicants, regulators, boards of management and the wider public, and
  2. providing a basis for target-setting to underpin continuous improvement of services through monitoring change over time and making comparisons with peer organisations.

Setting more specific objectives for monitoring performance is assisted by reference to the four Es (see p. 122 above).

The penultimate section of this chapter provides illustrative examples of ways in which social landlords have used performance monitoring to enhance their accountability and improve their performance in relation to the four Es. First, the information sources which social landlords may draw on in monitoring allocations performance and the types of monitoring most commonly found in practice are considered.

Monitoring in practice

One of the main requirements for performance monitoring is the availability of consistent and reliable information. While the existence of integrated IT systems and interrogation packages opens the door to innovative approaches to monitoring performance, in practice attention has focused on outputs from a number of standard data sources which landlords must produce to meet external requirements.

Standard data sources

Local authorities

For local authorities, the Operational Information Form, completed as part of the annual HIP process, collects a range of performance information including numbers of house-holds by type on the register, lettings and nominations (with family-size dwellings identified separately) and homeless acceptances. It also requires authorities to certify that they are complying with the CRE's *Code of Practice in Rented Housing*, which stresses the need for ERKM systems (see Chap. 7, pp. 117–119 and p. 131 below).

Monitoring data on lettings must also be published annually under the Citizen's Charter framework. This includes a breakdown of allocations by the rehousing route, as well as the average relet interval for properties let. Another relevant, externally imposed requirement is the completion of a quarterly homelessness return to the DETR (Section E1 of form P1E). This includes questions relating to homelessness enquiries and decisions, including ethnic origin and household type information, which can be useful for wider monitoring purposes. Information produced for the Annual Report to Tenants may also provide the basis for more general performance monitoring.

RSLs

RSLs are required to complete an Annual Regulatory Return which collects information on numbers of new lettings and relets of general needs and supported housing and on numbers of vacant units by reason and length of time vacant. As discussed in Chapter 6, RSLs must also self-certify that their selection and allocation policies are effectively controlled and accurately recorded.

Associations which own and manage more than 250 homes or hostel bedspaces are also required to fully participate in the Corporation's CORE system for new lettings, which includes a wide range of information on the applicant (including his or her income and ethnic origin), the property allocated, and the letting itself (e.g. relet interval). This provides a wealth of monitoring data for comparing performance, for example in relation to local authority nominations and proportions of

BME households housed. It is a particularly useful tool for local authorities working in partnership with RSLs operating in their area to jointly plan and monitor lettings.

Internal management information

In addition to the above externally influenced performance data, most landlords generate a considerable volume of data in connection with their allocations activities. Provided that it is collected and recorded consistently, this data can be used creatively to improve the housing service. Examples of the opportunities for monitoring of this sort are given below.

Housing registers

These can be used to generate detailed profiles of changing levels of expressed housing needs, and may be used to target a range of interventions such as housing advice, environmental health activity and LCHO, rather than simply acting as a 'waiting list' for social housing. Expressed demand on the housing register can also be compared with independent indicators of housing need such as the Census and local housing need studies and surveys. For example, the actual proportion of applicants from particular minority ethnic groups might be compared with expected levels based on the Census or needs surveys, which indicate relative levels of housing need of different groups.

Offers of accommodation

These may be monitored in relation to housing need, waiting times, locations, acceptance rates and reasons for refusal. Housing need and waiting times can be monitored by comparing offer data with housing register data. Are certain groups receiving less, or less speedy, offers than would be expected on the basis of their points levels? The location of offers can be compared with areas of choice specified by applicants to examine the extent to which offer procedures are maximising overall utility, and to generate useful waiting time data to inform future applicant choice. Variations in acceptance rates of offers can be explored in relation to area, property type etc. to identify the need for special allocation policies (see Chap. 4 for a discussion of local lettings initiatives).

Lettings

These can be monitored in relation to target relet times for properties to gain a picture of the relative efficiency of the allocations process. Such monitoring may be more useful where comparisons are made over time or with similar organisations. Overall lettings activity should usually be compared to expected performance using a lettings plan or similar policy framework. As noted above, there is a role for local partnerships of RSLs and local authorities to review lettings against a local lettings plan using the CORE data, local authority lettings data, and (where available) a CHR to give an overview of demand.

Benchmarking clubs

Increasing numbers of landlords are beginning to share information on performance with other organisations of a similar size and type and working in a similar context. For example, 56 stock transfer housing associations have formed a benchmarking club to exchange information on a broad range of cost and management information, including average relet times for different property types, tenancy turnover rates and staff costs attributable to allocations and lettings activities. By agreeing common definitions and standardising for context, such exercises can generate more useful performance data. Such comparisons are usually of the 'can opener' variety, enabling landlords to identify areas of variation between their performance and the peer group norm where further investigation may be required to understand the sources of variation and whether further action is required.

Performance indicators

Implicit in the above discussion is the concept of a performance standard or target against which actual performance
can be compared. Indicators and targets may be related to the
four Es (see p. 122 above). To be useful, performance indicators must reflect local objectives, context, circumstances and
administrative arrangements. Some illustrative examples are
included below.

Indicators of economy

Indicators of economy are concerned with the inputs such as
staff and money.

Staff figures (using Full Time Equivalents (FTEs)) may
be expressed in relation to any of the following comparators:
per thousand local population, enquiries, offers, applications
or tenancies—for example, FTE per thousand tenancies
involved in administering the housing register.

Input costs may be compared between different administrative arrangements. For example, landlords may wish to
ask whether CHRs are more economical than individual
waiting lists in total system costs by examining staffing costs
for administering application forms, data input, interviews
and home visits and monitoring such costs before and after
the establishment of a CHR—for example, cost per thousand
applicants for application forms, data input, interviews and
home visits.

Indicators of efficiency

These measure the relationship between inputs and outputs.

Target times

One of the most common types of efficiency indicator sets
timescales within which specified operations should normally

be performed. Such timescales often appear in contract specifications, as the first point below illustrates. Time standards are also found in national regulatory and good practice guidance, such as the DETR's *Code of Guidance on Allocations and Homelessness* from which the second point below is taken:

1. 'An allocation will be made and notified to the prospective tenant within x working days of the contractor providing a date for letting or within x days of a refusal as appropriate' (from King and Newbury, 1996).

2. 'Interview and carry out an initial assessment of the eligibility of the applicant on the day of the application … complete enquiries as quickly as possible and preferably within 30 working days … issue written decisions to the applicant within three working days of completion of enquiries' (draft revised *Code*, para. 9.16).

Void and occupancy rates

Another common form of efficiency indicator relevant to the allocations process compares usage rates with capacity, for example the percentage of properties empty by status and the reason why they are empty against the percentage of hostel bedspaces occupied.

Indicators of effectiveness

These are less concerned with 'good housekeeping' and more concerned with whether the policies' underlying objectives are being met. This requires objectives to be clearly specified. In the allocations arena there are two main methods which can be used to set targets against which actual lettings can be compared. Their appropriateness depends on the systems used to assess need and to prioritise applications.

Demand group/access route targets

These targets are widely used as a planning and monitoring tool by landlords who operate parallel systems for assessment and prioritisation of different categories of need or demand groups (e.g. transfers, new applicants and homeless). Each year the landlord estimates the likely supply of lettings (broken down by size of accommodation, area, etc.) and the likely needs of each demand group, and then sets targets for the number or proportion of each category of supply which should go to each group as a basis for monitoring performance.

Bypass monitoring

This is an alternative tool which may be more appropriate for landlords who use a single points scheme to prioritise all categories of housing need (a trend encouraged by the establishment of statutory housing registers under HA 1996). In theory, offers should be made to applicants with highest points totals qualified for and expressing an interest in properties of a particular size and in a particular area. Bypass monitoring is used to identify cases where the highest points applicants are bypassed and to identify the reasons for this. It is a good tool for accountability and is often used in internal audit reviews of lettings. Allocations officers may be required to keep records of the reasons for each bypass decision to create an audit trail which can be monitored after the event.

Non-needs objectives

In the 1990s, there has been an increase in the use of lettings policies which incorporate explicit criteria other than meeting housing need. Examples include controlling child densities and influencing neighbourhood social mix. As noted in Chapter 6, the Housing Corporation's *Performance Standards* allow RSLs to adopt local lettings policies which override the priority normally given to those in greatest need, where such policies have defined objectives aimed at preventing or tackling social problems. Such policies should not last for more than three years and must include 'arrangements for monitoring and reporting on progress in achieving objectives'.

Indicators of equity

These are broadly concerned with the 'fairness' of an allocations system and will usually seek to identify the impact of allocations processes on different sub-groups within the population (e.g. minority ethnic groups, single parents, older people, people with disabilities etc.). The remainder of this section focuses on ERKM as an example of equity indicators and targets.

Chapter 7 introduces the concept of ERKM as a means of ensuring that unlawful racial discrimination is avoided, and identifies the need to monitor each stage of the allocations process, including the quality of accommodation allocated. There has been considerable attention to the setting of race equality targets for allocations. Like the demand group targets discussed above, race equality targets are not quotas which must be met (such quotas would probably be illegal under the RRA), but rather expectations against which performance can be reviewed and the reasons for departures investigated.

Example: approaches to setting race equality targets

Simple targets

Source of information	1991 Census—ethnic origin breakdown
	Application list breakdown

More refined targets

Source of information	1991 Census—ethnic origin breakdown
	Other national data (e.g. General Household Survey)
	Application list breakdown
	Local surveys
	Needs analysis
	Other service details (e.g. void rates/availability)

Source: Jones (1996).

One very specific approach to performance monitoring of allocations (see the example below) is that employed by Birmingham City Council, which compares representation of different ethnic groups among lettings with their representation on the housing register using a performance indicator known as the 'Relative Success Rate' (RSR).

> **Example: Birmingham City Council—method for calculating Relative Success Rate**
>
> An RSR is calculated through the following five steps.
>
> **1.** Calculate the percentage of people from each ethnic group on the council waiting lists. Because the proportion of BME communities on the applicant and transfer lists differ considerably, each list is considered separately (only pointed cases are included).
>
> **2.** Calculate the *actual* number of lettings made to each group from the applicant list and the transfer list.
>
> **3.** Calculate the number of lettings which *would* have been made to each group, had they received lettings in proportion to their representation on the two waiting lists. This can be considered as the *expected* number of lettings for each group.
>
> **4.** Add together the actual number of lettings from the applicant list and the transfer list, and add together the expected number of lettings from each list.
>
> **5.** Divide the *total number of actual lettings* by the *total number of expected lettings* and multiplying by 100.
>
> An RSR value of 100 indicates that a particular group has received 100 per cent of the lettings one would expect given the group's proportion of the waiting list. An RSR value of less than 100 means that the group is receiving fewer lettings than expected, whilst an RSR value higher than 100 indicates a higher success rate than would be expected.

The CRE's *Code of Practice in Rented Housing* recommends that the main components of an effective monitoring system should include: 'Monitoring ethnic records on a regular basis with analytical reports produced at a minimum of every six months for most organisations.' Meanwhile Jones (1996) has noted that:

> 'Agencies serving communities with small black and minority ethnic populations may not need to produce monitoring reports so frequently. In such areas an annual report may suffice. This is not to say, however, that ethnic monitoring data need only be looked at once a year. If such data has been integrated into "mainstream" information systems then it should be looked at with the same frequency as other management information.'

Fraudulent applications

One aspect of auditing may be to check for fraudulent applications for housing. To deter abuse, such applications, whether under Part VI (allocations) or Part VII (homelessness) of HA 1996, may give rise to the commission of a criminal offence. The three offences—making a false statement, withholding information, and failure to notify changes in circumstances— may be committed in respect of applications to local authorities and not in respect of *direct* applications to RSLs.

Both HA 1985 (governing secure tenancies) and HA 1988 (governing assured tenancies) include grounds for possession where a fraudulent statement has been made.

The criminal offences

Each of the offences is prosecuted in the magistrates' court and carries a maximum fine of level 5 on the standard scale. In order to prove an offence a prosecutor must establish the case beyond reasonable doubt, as opposed to the civil standard of balance of probabilities.

Making false statement

This offence is committed by anyone—not only an applicant—
who knowingly or recklessly makes a statement which:

1. in the case of a Part VI application, is false in a material
   particular (HA 1996, s. 171(1)); or
2. in the case of a Part VII application, is false in a material
   particular with intent to induce an authority to believe
   that the person making the statement or any other
   person is homeless, threatened with homelessness, has
   a priority need, or did not become homeless or threatened with homelessness intentionally (HA 1996,
   s. 214(1)).

In each case intent must be shown, in that the maker of the
statement must *know* that it is false or must be *reckless* as to
whether it is true. A statement made in all innocence therefore
is not incriminating.

Withholding information

Again, this offence is committed by anyone who knowingly
withholds information which the authority has reasonably
required him or her to give in connection with the exercise of
its functions under Parts VI and VII (HA 1996, ss. 171(1) and
214(1)). This offence has a wide ambit and conceivably can
include a case where an authority has requested information
from, for example, a relative or former landlord. Under the
Part VII offence, an intent must be shown to induce the authority to believe that the person withholding the information or
any other person is entitled to accommodation or assistance.

Failure to notify changes

This offence arises only in relation to Part VII and may be
committed only by an applicant. An applicant is under a
positive duty to inform the authority as soon as possible of
any change of facts material to his or her application, which
occurs before receipt of notification of its decision on the

application (s. 214(2)). Of particular difficulty is the issue of what constitutes a 'material change of facts'. In accordance with the usual principles of criminal law, the courts should interpret the provisions narrowly, in favour of the accused.

Authorities are *required* (s. 214(3)) to explain the duty to an applicant 'in ordinary language' and additionally to explain that failure to notify a material change is a criminal offence. At paragraph 9.14 of the DETR's draft revised *Code of Guidance*, it is suggested that 'this needs to be done sensitively so as not to intimidate the applicant, and at the earliest opportunity'. It is a defence for the applicant to show that no explanation was given by the authority or, alternatively, that there was a reasonable excuse for non-compliance.

Grounds for possession

Where a tenancy has been granted as the result of giving a false statement, grounds for possession are provided against both secure and assured tenants. These are contained in Ground 5 of Schedule 2 to HA 1985 and Ground 17 of Schedule 2 to HA 1988. In each case, the ground is identical and is that the 'tenant is the person, or one of the persons, to whom the tenancy was granted and the landlord was induced to grant the tenancy by a false statement made knowingly or recklessly by … the tenant, or … a person acting at the tenant's instigation'.

In order for the ground to be made out, the landlord must be *induced* to grant the tenancy by the false statement; therefore, a statement which would have made no difference to the allocation or which was patently false would probably not qualify.

If a person other than the tenant makes the statement, they must have been instigated to do so by the tenant; therefore, a false statement which is made without the tenant's participation (e.g. by a former landlord) would not give a reason for possession.

In the case of both grounds it must, additionally, be shown that it is 'reasonable' to order possession. In general, the issue of reasonableness is very wide: for Grounds 5 and 17, the judge is entitled to take into account the policy of discouraging deceitful applications for housing which result in others having to wait longer for accommodation (*Rushcliffe BC v Watson* (1991)).

Removal from housing register

By section 163(5) of HA 1996, authorities are given discretion to 'remove a person from their housing register in such circumstances as they think fit', and they *must* do so if it appears that he or she has never been a qualifying person or is no longer such a person. Subject to complying with the notice requirements, it would be open to an authority to formulate a policy whereby a person who has made a false statement might be penalised by being removed from the list.

Summary

Recent years have seen increased emphasis on monitoring the operation of allocations systems. To a large extent, this has been stimulated by new regulatory requirements on social landlords and has been facilitated by developments in IT.

Other than the need to respond to regulatory obligations, monitoring of allocations is mainly inspired by the need to promote accountability and to ensure that systems are delivering the four Es.

Social landlords are making increasing use of internal administrative information as key monitoring data. Such data is collected in the context of a number of activities central to the allocations process (e.g. management of housing registers, property lettings). This places a heavy emphasis on the need to collect and record operational data consistently and to develop IT systems capable of data aggregation and analysis as well as meeting day-to-day administrative requirements.

Particular measures of activity related to allocations are relevant to monitoring with respect to each of the four Es.

Fraudulent housing applications are covered by the criminal law, and there are specific grounds on which housing applicants may be prosecuted in relation to both Parts VI and VII of HA 1996. There are also specific grounds for repossession of properties where a tenancy has been granted and it subsequently comes to light that this is the result of a fraudulent application.

Further reading

Chartered Institute of Housing (1995). *Housing Management Standards Manual*. Coventry: CIH.

Department of the Environment, Transport and the Regions (2000). *Code of Guidance on the Allocation of Accommodation and Homelessness*. London: Stationery Office.

Goss, S. and Blackaby, R. (1998). *Designing Local Housing Strategies—A Good Practice Guide*. Coventry: CIH/Local Government Association.

Jones, A. (1996). *Making Monitoring Work: A Handbook for Racial Equality Practitioners*. Coventry: Centre for Research in Ethnic Relations, University of Warwick.

King, A. and Newbury, J. (1996). *Managing Housing Contracts*. Coventry: Chartered Institute of Housing.

Mullins, D. (1991). *Accounting For Equality—A Handbook on Ethnic Monitoring in Housing*. London: CRE.

National Federation of Housing Associations (1985). *Ethnic Record Keeping and Monitoring*. London: NFHA.

Index

Also available in Arden's Housing Library

Houses in Multiple Occupation
Law and practice in the management of social housing
Andrew Dymond, Barrister

The law can ensure that houses in multiple occupation provide safe, comfortable housing at a reasonable price. This book helps those working for this aim with clear and concise guidance on the general and special powers available to local authorities including:
- The establishment of registration schemes.
- Powers to serve and enforce notices on owners or managers to remedy unsafe conditions, overcrowding, poor repair or badly management.
- Standards that should be maintained and assistance available.
- Duties in relation to common problems associated with HMOs.
- Responsibilities for rehousing and compensation.

Chapter contents
Definitions • Registration Schemes • Conditions, Facilities and Overcrowding • Enforcement • Paying for Repairs and Improvements • Day-to-day Management and Occupiers' Rights • Rehousing Tenants

About the Author
Andrew Dymond is a barrister and member of Arden Chambers. He is also the author of *Security of Tenure* and *Presenting Possession Proceedings*, also published in Arden's Housing Library.

ISBN: 1-090001-10-2
Published Spring 2000
Available directly from Plymbridge Distributors Ltd. Tel. 01752 202301 or Fax 01752 202333

Also available in Arden's Housing Library

Security of Tenure
Law and practice in the management of social housing
Second edition
Andrew Dymond, Barrister

This completely revised and up-to-date edition explains in accessible language the legal framework within which a housing manager is working on any given case, demonstrating the options available in the management of a tenancy. An appendix includes all required model letters and forms for use in casework. Guidance in key areas is given including:
- Procedures for creating different kinds of tenancy.
- Identifying which Act applies to the tenancy.
- What rights exist to remain in the property.
- The circumstances in which security of tenure may be lost.
- The powers landlords have to terminate the tenancy.
- Procedures for termination by the landlord and re-gaining possession.

Chapter contents
Status of the Occupier • Tenant or Licensee? • Secure and Assured Tenancies • Conditions for Security of Tenure • Seeking Possession • Grounds for Possession Against Secure Tenants • Grounds for Possession Against Assured Tenants • Suitable Alternative Accommodation • Reasonableness • Other Occupiers • Possession Orders • Termination by the Tenant

About the Author
Andrew Dymond is a barrister and member of Arden Chambers. He is also the author of *Presenting Possession Proceedings*, also published in Arden's Housing Library.

ISBN: 1-898001-63-4
Published Spring 2000
Available directly from Plymbridge Distributors Ltd. Tel. 01752 202301 or Fax 01752 202333

Also available in Arden's Housing Library

Discrimination and Social Housing
Law and practice in the management of social housing
Alyson Kilpatrick, Barrister

This book is a tool for making real the objectives of the anti-discrimination legislation on sex, race and disability. Clearly spelling out the practical implications of the codes of guidance and the law—including the new Human Rights Act—the book is as helpful in establishing where positive action is legitimate as it is in pointing out indirectly discriminatory practices. Access to accommodation, housing management issues, as well as selection and employment of staff are all covered; guidance by the author is provided on all key problems including:

- How to assess allegations and legal responsibility for unfair treatment on grounds of race, sex or disability.
- Responsibility to tackle harassment.
- Responsibility to have fair treatment in relation to recruitment, selection, employment and dismissal.

Chapter contents
Legal Framework • Enforcement of the Legislation • Discrimination on Grounds of Race or Sex • Disability • Sexual Orientation • General Public Duties • Monitoring • Housing Services • Housing Allocation and Homeless • Dealing with Harassment • Discrimination in Employment.

About the Author
Alyson Kilpatrick is a barrister and member of Arden Chambers. She is the author of *Repairs and Maintenance*, also published in Arden's Housing Library.

ISBN: 1-898001-34-0
Published Spring 2000
Available directly from Plymbridge Distributors Ltd. Tel 01752-202301 or Fax 01752 202333

Also available in Arden's Housing Library

Unauthorised and Temporary Occupiers
Law and practice in the management of social housing
Lydia Challen, Barrister

This book explains the legal status of residents whose occupation is either
temporary or has not been authorised, the rights they have, and how
these can be brought to an end. Particular emphasis is given to showing
how the rights to occupy property can be affected by the occurrence of
different events. The law and its application to common management
problems, such as disrepair and nuisance, is set out. The question of how
empty property can be used without creating security of tenure is
considered. Even if security is conferred there may still be grounds for
regaining possession and details given of the different sorts of possession
proceedings, when they are appropriate and how they should be brought.

Chapter contents
Policy Issues Relating to Housing Use • Giving Use with Security • Giving
Use without Security • Liability for Premises • Classes of Occupation •
Statutory Protection and Security • Termination of Rights of Occupation •
Common Management Problems • Summary Proceedings • Interim
Possession Proceedings • Injunctive Proceedings • Ordinary Possession
Proceedings • Criminal Proceedings • Private and Public Law Defences •
Preparing Possession Proceedings • Removal Directions and Orders •
Summary Proceedings and Police Action.

About the Author
Lydia Challen is a barrister employed by a London firm of Solicitors, and
formerly a member of Arden Chambers.

ISBN: 1-898001-50-2
Published Spring 2000
Available directly from Plymbridge Distributors Ltd. Tel 01752 202301 or
Fax 01752 202333

Also available in Arden's Housing Library

RSL Finance and Rents
Law and practice in the management of social housing
William Okoya, Barrister

The financial environment in which registered social landlords (RSL)
operate is complex: on the one hand heavily regulated and
proceduralised, and on the other, commercial and competitive. This new
book in Arden's Housing Library explains the legal framework and
structures consistent with the need to become more commercial whilst
providing decent affordable homes for people in need. Accessible
guidance is given on all key issues including:
- What systems and resources must be in place to comply with regulatory
  requirements.
- How to make applications and bids for special grants and funding.
- How to deal with the consequences of various types of private finance.
- What policies and procedures should be used for rent setting and
  collection.
- How to deal with liabilities for corporation tax, capital gains tax, non-
  domestic rates, stamp duty and VAT.

Chapter contents
Registered Social Landlords • Regulatory Framework • Public Subsidy and
Finance of RSLs • Private Finance and Investment in RSLs • Rent and
Housing Benefit • Taxation • Mergers and acquisitions, group structures,
and partnerships and consortia.

About the Author
William Okoya is a barrister and member of Arden Chambers.

ISBN: 1-898001-52-9
Published Spring 2000
Available directly from Plymbridge Distributors Ltd. Tel 01752 202301 or
Fax 01752 202333

Also available in Arden's Housing Library

Children and Housing
Law and practice in the management of social housing
Josephine Henderson, Barrister

All children need to be adequately housed, but there is a variety of ways in which this may be achieved, and problems to which this may give rise. Thus some children need to be housed with their parents, and to house the children may require rehousing the whole family. On the other hand, some children may not have any support from their family, may have left home, or may be in the care of the local authority. In this case, very different considerations may arise in seeking to provide adequate housing. What can and should authorities and other landlords provide for the individual child? What are the legal consequences of providing housing for children. Once housed it may be that children are in fact a problem (e.g. through anti-social behaviour), or that although housing is provided it is not adequate for the child (e.g. because the child is disabled, or because the condition of the house makes the child ill). This book addresses these practical problems and many others in providing comprehensive coverage of housing issues as they affect children.

Chapter contents
Assessments under the Housing Act 1996, Part VII • Accommodation provision under the Housing Act 1996, Part VII • Key duties to provide accommodation and other services under the Children Act 1989 • Assessments under the Children Act • Accommodation provision under the Children Act • Responsibility for children in care and young people who have left care • Benefits and grants available to young people, families and housing providers • Duties to co-operate imposed on housing and social services authorities • Methods of resolving disputes

About the Author
Josephine Henderson is a barrister and member of Arden Chambers. She is the author of *Rights to Buy and Acquire*, also published in Arden's Housing Library.

ISBN: 1-898001-20-0
Published Spring 2000
Available directly from Plymbridge Distributors Ltd. Tel 01752-202301 or Fax 01752-202333

Also available in Arden's Housing Library

Tied Accommodation
Law and practice in the management of social housing
Dominic Preston, Barrister

This book explains the rights, responsibilities and housing management issues in dealing with staff living in accommodation as part of their employment ñ such as caretakers and teachers in schools, wardens in sheltered accommodation, social workers, park-keepers and others. Guidance is given on all key problem areas including:
- How to distinguish a tenancy from a licence.
- How to distinguish a service tenancy from service occupancies under the Housing Act 1985 and the Housing Act 1988.
- How introductory tenancies are created and terminated. Special grounds for possession of a secure tenancy.
- How to terminate assured and assured shorthold tenancies.
- How to terminate fixed term and periodic tenancies.
- How to terminate non-secure licences. Possession and dismissal.
- How to deal with right to buy or acquire; disrepair; rent increases; variation of rent and dismissal.

Chapter contents
Tenancy or Licence? • Categories of Tied Occupier. • Secure Tenants and Licensees. • Assured Tenants. • Termination of Non-secure Tenancies. • Termination of Non-secure Licences. • Housing Management Issues.

About the Author
Dominic Preston is a barrister and member of Arden Chambers.

ISBN: 1-898001-49-9
Published Spring 2000
Available directly from Plymbridge Distributors Ltd. Tel 01752 202301 or Fax 01752 202333

Also available in Arden's Housing Library

A Guide to the Planning Process
Law and practice in the management of social housing
Iain Colville, Barrister

This book provides practical legal guidance on the steps that must be taken from the first day it has been decided to carry out any housing development to the day on which the decision of the authority is finally resolved. Issues on which guidance is given include:
- How an authority should prepare a development plan and how RSLs can be involved.
- What types of work require planning permission?
- How to proceed with the application, steps to take before and after it is made.
- What an authority can and cannot take into account when determining the application.
- How appeals are made procedure and the steps to be followed by parties involved.
- Powers and procedures to deal with development carried out without consent.
- Powers to protect the environment.

Chapter contents
The Development Plan • The Meaning of 'Development' • The Planning Application • The Determination • Inquiries and Appeals • Enforcement Powers • Special Controls

About the Author
Iain Colville is a practising barrister specialising in local planning and is a member of Arden Chambers.

ISBN: 1-898001-51-0
Published Spring 2000
Available directly from Plymbridge Distributors Ltd. Tel 01752 202301 or Fax 01752 202333

Also available in Arden's Housing Library

Repairs and Maintenance
Law and practice in the management of social housing
Alyson Kilpatrick, Barrister

'An admirably concise and thorough exposition of the principles of the law in this area.' *Housing Agenda*

Housing staff need a practical understanding of the landlord's legal repair obligations and those of their tenants. Illustrated with examples of various types of complaint, this book explains the possible responses and the powers to get work done when action is required by law. There is a step-by-step guide to the role of housing staff if disputed matters go to court. Includes checklists and sample legal documents.

Chapter contents
Social Landlord's Contractual Liabilities • Common Types of Complaint • Tenants' Remedies • Public Health Duties • Tenants' Contractual Obligations • Getting the Works Done • Improvements • Court Proceedings • Compendium of Damages Awards

About the Author
Alyson Kilpatrick is a barrister at Arden Chambers and specialises in housing, landlord and tenant, environmental health, local government, employment, social security and EC law. She is the author of *Discrimination in Housing* (also published in Arden's Housing Library) and editor, *Housing Encyclopaedia, Housing Law Report* and *Journal of Housing Law.*

ISBN 1-898001-11-1
Published 1996
Available directly from Plymbridge Distributors Ltd. Tel 01752 202301 or Fax 01752 202333

Also available in Arden's Housing Library

Dealing with Disrepair
A manager's guide to inspection and diagnosis
Patrick Reddin, FRICS, FBEng

'**The technical information is simply and clearly presented with useful building diagrams ... its methodical approach will make it particularly useful as a training tool for both landlord and tenant.**'
Housing Agenda

'**This book should make a valuable contribution to raising standards and customer care, efficiency and effectiveness.**' *Simon Pott, past president of the RICS*

Housing managers need to understand the buildings their tenants are living in, accurately define what repair is required and know how to get the work done. Breaking new ground, this book describes in lay terms building structures and materials—and what can go wrong. There is step-by-step guidance on what to look for and how to carry out an inspection, as well as methods of reporting findings of disrepair. Over 30 detailed cross-section drawings of houses are included.

Chapter contents
Elements of a House • Construction Materials • Enemies of Healthy Buildings • Preparing for Inspections • Carrying Out Inspections • Compiling Reports • Assessing Priorities • Follow-up Priorities • Court Proceedings

About the Author
Patrick Reddin is a Fellow of the Royal Institution of Chartered Surveyors and the senior partner of Reddin & Nuttal, London. He specialises in the diagnosis and rectification of building defects, including housing disrepair. His experience extends over 30 years.

ISBN 1-898001-06-5
Published 1996
Available directly from Plymbridge Distributors Ltd. Tel 01752 202301 or Fax 01752 202333

Also available in Arden's Housing Library

Rights to Buy and Acquire

Law and practice in the management of social housing
Josephine Henderson, Barrister

'This book will be essential reading and reference for any housing professional with the task of administering sales to tenants ... the step-by-step guide to procedure in Chapter 4 is worth the purchase price by itself.' *Agenda*

As problems surface from the early burst of sales activity of council homes an accessible guide to the legal process that underpins these tenants' rights has been lacking: this book fills the gap. In addition to guidance on the Right to Buy their homes that council and some housing association tenants have had for nearly 20 years, the Right to Acquire for the tenants of housing associations and other registered social landlords is also explained.

Chapter contents
Who has the Right to Buy? • Qualifications and Exceptions • What is Bought? • Procedure • The Price and Paying It • The Grant or Conveyance • Loss and Enforcement of Right to Buy • Changes in the Landlord's Interest • Extension of Right • Housing Associations and Other Registered Social Landlords

About the Author
Josephine Henderson is a barrister at Arden Chambers and specialises in housing, landlord and tenant, environmental health, employment, family and child law. She is the author of *Children and Housing*, also published in Arden's Housing Library.

ISBN 1-898001-19-7
Published June 1997
Available directly from Plymbridge Distributors Ltd. Tel 01752 202301 or Fax 01752 202333

Also available in Arden's Housing Library

Leaseholder Management
Law and practice in the management of social housing
Desmond Kilcoyne, Barrister

For social housing landlords, today's leaseholder is often yesterday's
tenant. And although their rights and obligations have changed, they
certainly have not disappeared—and nor have housing problems. This
guide provides a comprehensive explanation of what those legal rights
and obligations are, and with scarce resources, this understanding is
crucial for the task of helping to meet leaseholders' expectations while still
delivering a service to tenants.

Chapter contents
Leaseholders, Leaseholds and Leases • The Legal Framework • Service
and Annual Charges • The Statutory Law • Service Charges: major works •
Service Charges and Improvement Contributions: right to buy leases •
Recovery of Service Charges • Covenants and Regulation of Management
• Remedies of Landlord and Leaseholder • Change of Leaseholder or
Landlord • Security of Tenure • Enfranchisement and Extension of Long
Lease • Right of First Refusal

About the Author
Desmond Kilcoyne is a barrister at Arden Chambers and specialises in
housing, landlord and tenant, mortgages and real property. He is a
contributor to *Atkin's Court Forms*.

ISBN 1-898001-10-3
Published December 1997
Available directly from Plymbridge Distributors Ltd. Tel 01752 202301 or
Fax 01752 202333

Also available in Arden's Housing Library

Tenants' Rights
Law and practice in the management of social housing
Caroline Hunter, Barrister

'Caroline Hunter has written very clearly and concisely and made extremely good use of case law.' *The Adviser*

Secure tenants of councils and housing associations have more control over their homes than ever before—and keeping abreast of these rights is essential for housing professionals. This guide covers rights to succession, taking in lodgers, exchanging homes and subletting. Tenants' collective rights to information, to manage, to change their landlord are also included.

Chapter contents
Historical Background • Succession • Assignment, Lodgers and Subletting • Changing the Terms of the Tenancy • Information and Consultation • The Right to Manage • Estate Redevelopment

About the Author
Caroline Hunter lectures at the University of Nottingham and is a barrister at Arden Chambers. She specialises in housing, landlord and tenant, local government powers, finance and proceedings, competitive tendering and environmental health. She is the author (with Andy Selman) of *CCT of Housing Management* and (with Kerry Bretherton) of *Anti-social Behaviour* (Arden's Housing Library), and also many other specialist practitioner works including Arden & Hunter's *Local Government Finance Law and Practice*.

ISBN 1-898001-13-8
Published 1995
Available directly from Plymbridge Distributors Ltd. Tel 01752 202301 or Fax 01752 202333

Also available in Arden's Housing Library

Anti-social Behaviour
Law and practice in the management of social housing
Caroline Hunter, Barrister and Kerry Bretherton, Barrister

Anti-social behaviour is a growing problem that is taxing housing managers and others. This new book looks at remedies available for landlords against tenants and other perpetrators, as well as setting out the landlord's liability to third parties. Special treatment is given to specific problems such as violence, drug dealing, pets, noise, and behaviour motivated by prejudice. Guidance is given on the practical problems involved in enforcement and bringing cases to court.

Chapter contents
Providing a Comprehensive Approach • Liability of the Landlord for Anti-social Behaviour • Introductory Tenancies • Nuisance Behaviour by Tenants • Nuisance Behaviour by Particular Groups • Specific Problems • Behaviour Motivated by Prejudice • In Court

About the Authors
Caroline Hunter is a barrister at Arden Chambers and lectures at the University of Nottingham. She specialises in housing, landlord and tenant, local government powers, finance and proceedings, competitive tendering and environmental health. She is the author of *Tenants' Rights* and, with Andy Selman, *CCT of Housing Management* (Arden's Housing Library) and many other specialist practitioner works including Arden & Hunter's *Local Government Finance Law and Practice*.
        Kerry Bretherton is a barrister at Arden Chambers and specialises in housing, landlord and tenant, and environmental health.

ISBN 1-898001-37-5
Published 1998
Available directly from Plymbridge Distributors Ltd. Tel 01752 202301 or Fax 01752 202333

Also available in Arden's Housing Library

Presenting Possession Proceedings
Law and practice in the management of social housing
Andrew Dymond, Barrister

'Housing managers and officers involved in regaining possession should find this book invaluable.' *ADC Review*

With pressure to maximise rent and minimise management costs, more and more housing managers are finding themselves handling possession proceedings. This book provides expert guidance through that process: how to gather evidence and begin the proceedings; how to use pre-trial and trial court procedures and what orders to apply for. Checklists and model forms are included to make sure proceedings do not run into the sand because of error or omission.

Chapter contents
Commencing Possession Proceedings • What Needs to be Proved? • The Return Date • Pre-Trial Procedure • Evidence • The Trial • Rent Arrears Cases • Other Types of Possession Action • Possession Orders • Further Action • Court Forms

About the Author
Andrew Dymond is a barrister at Arden Chambers and specialises in housing, landlord and tenant, environmental health and social security. He is author of *Security of Tenure* and *Houses in Multiple Occupation* (Arden's Housing Library) and editor, *Housing Encyclopaedia, Housing Law Reports* and *Journal of Housing Law*.

ISBN 1-898001-15-4
Published 1996
Available directly from Plymbridge Distributors Ltd. Tel 01752 202301 or Fax 01752 202333